APOCALYPTIC GRACE

THE EVOLUTION OF CULTURE AND CONSCIOUSNESS

Stephen Powell's *Apocalyptic Grace* is important for anyone wanting to understand the deep background to diversity consciousness and conflict work. His work advances what is presently known as multicultural psychology, which is the psychology of our present and future planet.

Arnold Mindell, *The Shaman's Body*

This is an exquisitely crafted collection of material on cultural diversity that illuminates ideas we've been circling around for a long time.

Kaylynn Sullivan TwoTrees, *Somebody Always Singing You*

Powell looks deeply into how cultures have shifted the past 50,000 years. *Apocalyptic Grace* is thick with well-researched and thought-provoking passages. A synthesis of new thought and old prophesies, it holds just the explanation we need now to understand the shifts happening in our collective experience and personal lives.

Cindy Bellinger, *Enchantment Magazine*

Hear and feel the beat of Stephen Powell as he calls us to dance toward the apocalyptic grace within ourselves.

Bradford Keeney, *Shaking Medicine: The Healing Power of Ecstatic Movement*

STEPHEN POWELL, MA, LMHC

APOCALYPTIC GRACE

THE EVOLUTION OF CULTURE AND CONSCIOUSNESS

OCEAN TREE BOOKS
Santa Fe, New Mexico

For information, contact:

Stephen Powell
County Rd. 12, #40, Espanola, NM 87532
(505) 927-3747
wildmtngoat@windstream.net

Medicine Wheel Mandala on cover is designed by Rose Morton, copyright © 2004. Rose Morton is a master herbologist and artist. Her photos are not so much technical as emotional and observational. She based this image on the native medicine wheel using barley, peas, beans, different types of corn, wheat and other seeds.

OCEAN TREE BOOKS

P. O. Box 1295, Santa Fe, NM 87504 (505) 983-1412 www.oceantree.com
Printed in Canada.

ISBN: 978-0943734-49-1

Library of Congress CIP data:

Powell, Stephen, 1956-
 Apocalyptic grace : the evolution of culture and consciousness / Stephen Powell.
   p.   cm.
 Includes bibliographical references and index.
 ISBN 978-0-943734-49-1 (alk. paper)
 1. Human evolution. 2. Human behavior. 3. Social evolution. 4. Ethnopsychology.
 5. Consciousness. I. Title.
 GN281.4.P67 2010
 304--dc22
 2009032130

Dedication

This work must honor the many teachers, mentors, and soul partners who have come into my life, including Roshi Joan Halifax, Kaylynn Sullivan TwoTrees, Robert Waterman, Steven Foster and Meredith Little, Onye Onyemaechi, Don Chavez, Treaca Allen, and all of the countless students and clients that have grounded my ideas with their experience.

Acknowledgements

So many valued people and institutions contributed to this work. First, please forgive me for overlooking those who I may have unintentionally missed.

Special gratitude to Rebecca O'Day, my student, friend and first-round editor who convinced me of the textbook value of this book. To my ongoing support network: Laurel Chiten, Mark Garland, Thalia Jackson, Ian Bald and family, John Stevens, Lauren Moore, Laurie McDonald and Judy Sher. To my "landmates" Shibli Fazal and Fermin Lopez, who kept my farm going while I was preoccupied. To my Montana family, Beverly and Mary Jo, and to Beverly Kune who helps put me back together after my epic breakdowns/breakthroughs.

To my many fellow travelers in Christ, including Pastor Kevin and The LightHouse Church of Chimayo, Pastor Eva and Fruit of the Spirit Ministries of Santa Fe, the mentorship of Jimmie Orr and the staff at the Vineyard Church in Santa Fe; to Leroi, Carolyn and Justice and the incredible spiritual family they've created in my Espanola community; to my neighbor and brother Titus and the men's group "the Fight Club" I've been asked to help recreate.

To Rose Morton, who graduated with honors as a master herbologist, makes her own smudge sticks and medicines, and creates mandalas from seeds and other natural materials, as you see in her brilliant rendition for the cover.

To my colleague Wendy Goodman; to my Santa Fe Community College supervisors Bruno Bornet and Bernadette Jacobs, who afforded me the opportunity to develop this material over the course of the last 15 years; to the faculty of Southwestern college in Santa Fe; to the Upaya Zen Center people and their openness to allow me to show up "as needed."

To my family who have accepted my role as the stray sheep, and to the trio that persevered with my "sensitive artist dogmas" in completing this project: publisher and old friend Richard Polese, editor Cinny Green, and layout designer B.J. Harris. And finally to the many four-legged friends -- horses, goats, dogs and cats -- who continue to demonstrate the power of unconditional love.

Contents

Preface

*A*pocalyptic Grace provides an anthropological model by which to understand multicultural psychology. This model addresses both past and present cultures, as well as how multicultural psychology continues to operate *within us*. As complex as this whole subject may seem, the journey of Cultural Anthropology tells us that humanity has had only four basic types of cultures: hunting and gathering, horticulture, agrarian, industrial. The disciplines of Archetypal Psychology and Comparative Religion will help us fill in the dynamics of each of these types of cultures, particularly in regard to how they continue to show up in the modern psyche.

In this work, these respective types of culture will be referred to as "Worlds." Psychologically speaking, each of us is our own unique mixture of these older Worlds and the modern mindset. In other words, even though most of us are in some manner a part of industrial culture, our inner sensibilities point back to ancient ways of experiencing life. Put all of this together and *Apocalyptic Grace* is about *The Evolution of Culture and Consciousness*. As prophecies and wisdom traditions have been forecasting from around the world, we are now bumping up against a Fifth World.

This helps explain the title, *Apocalyptic Grace*. While the notion of may seem rather "doom 'n' gloom," it is actually derived from the Greek word *apokalypsis* meaning "revelation, disclosure, unveiling." Like the overall nature of evolution, without tension and crisis there is no opportunity for viable change. As is regularly touted in the field of Recovery Psychology and praise and worship oriented Christianity, two of my own personal anchors, our mess becomes the message, our breakdown the breakthrough. Apocalypse, in other words, is not just what prophecies have forecasted as happening *out there*. Apocalypse is foremost an internal process by which circumstances bring us to our knees. From there, a true psychological growth and expansion is possible.

The tensions of global economic recession, ecological disaster, international and interpersonal conflicts invite deeper and novel resolution. So do the challenges of one's personal psychology. This work is not about looking at these tensions with a new kind of rose-colored glasses, but taking off our ethnocentric blinders and integrating the rich diversity that the journey of culture and psychology has been about. When and how this resolution actually arrives, both culturally and personally, has its own timing—that is, a matter of grace.

Because of the metaphoric quality of this journey, the disciplines of Anthropology, Psychology, and Comparative Religion have been moved to rely on central metaphors to explore and describe the human condition and story. And so it is in the long list of 20th century explorers of human nature. For mythologist Joseph Campbell (1959), this was "the journey of the hero;" for Jung and subsequent Jungians, it is "individuation;" and for Aldous Huxley's it was the study of comparative mysticism he entitled *The Perennial Philosophy* (1944).

In later generations, Ken Wilber (1980) described this journey as *The Atman Project*, a Hindu notion in which the individual soul becomes aligned with a universal soul. Jungian renegade Arnold Mindell (1985) referred to this process as "the dreambody," those seemingly irrational elements of the human experience that actually serve to make it whole.

Anthropologist Victor Turner (1982) turned to the concept of *communitas* and *liminality*, that constant ritual process by which we attempt to transcend, at least momentarily, our cherished social identities for a greater and expanding understanding of who we really are. Social theorist Michel Foucault (1980) referred to consciousness as being governed by *discourse*, meaning the rules and contexts beneath the surface of social and personal realities. Scholar of Comparative Religion Mircea Eliade (1978) noted that all beliefs seemed to center around a need for regeneration and core values and perceptions (*axis mundi*).

The Dallas School of Thomas Moore (1992), James Hillman (1975), and Robert Sardello (1999) entertained the sweeping territories of *psyche* and *soul,* by which the human personality was only the pawn of much deeper forces. Robert Moore (1992) and Robert Bly (2001) engaged similar material and were responsible for helping to launch the modern day Men's Movement.

While *Apocalyptic Grace* is written more for the layperson than the academic, I find it important at the outset to pay homage to all of these teachers and the global wisdom traditions they have engaged. At the center of this work is the notion of archetype, those particular psychological dynamics that seem to govern individuals, nations, and cultures alike.

Very little of our archetypal histories can be discarded. They are a part of our hardwiring. But they can be reinvested with new energies and possibilities. Jolande Jacobi, a student of Jung and the only one to receive sanctioned permission from Jung himself to write a primer for his work, shared these thoughts during World War II, our last full planetary apocalyptic outbreak:

> *Not without reason have the archetypal images and experiences always formed a central part of all of the religions of the earth. And although they have often been overlaid by dogma and stripped of their original form, they are still active in the psyche, their rich meaning is still powerfully at work, especially where religious faith remains a living force... Only where faith and dogma have frozen into empty forms—and this is largely the case in our ultra-civilized technological, rational minded Western world—have they lost their magic power and left man helpless and alone... However, in every individual psyche they can awaken to new life, exert their magic power, and condense into a kind of 'individual mythology,' which presents an impressive parallel to the great traditional mythologies of all peoples and epochs, concretizing as it were their origin, essence, meaning, and throwing new light on them. (Jacobi, The Psychology of C.G. Jung, 1942)*

Apocalyptic Grace is a journey into the cultural evolution of archetype, not as a linear march through time, but as strands of perennial wisdoms that continue to spiral back through the trials and triumphs of the human experience.

INTRODUCTION
Understanding Cultural Diversity

WORLD
THREE
Agrarian Hierarchy
circa 3500 BCE

WORLD
TWO
Horticultural
circa 10,000 BCE

WORLD
FOUR
Industrial
circa 1600s

WORLD
ONE
Hunting & Gathering
circa 50,000 BCE

Ancient Prophecy Meets Cultural Anthropology

My mother is German Baptist. My father is Polish Jew. When they were married in 1945, one side of my heritage was mass murdering the other side back on the European continent. While both sides of the family were already two generations removed from this tragedy, the deeper tragedy remained embedded within my thoughts. What is it about the human species—with all its dazzling array of cultural diversity and wisdom traditions—that allows this to happen? I moved around a lot in my twenties: Philadelphia, Montreal, Colorado. But wherever I went, these thoughts became a *karmic attraction*. If your family went through the Nazi Holocaust, I was attracted to you, as three girlfriends in a row would testify.

A major psychological point was being made. Whatever has not been worked out on the inside, will manifest and persist in the world. To break this pattern, one option would be to airlift the participants of war into a psychotherapist's office. Considering the unlikelihood of that endeavor, the next best solution seemed to start working this stuff out on the inside. This led to a study of how the cultural, psychological and spiritual differences of humanity came about. The result was a synthesis of the three disciplines in which I received college degrees—Cultural Anthropology, Comparative Religion, and Archetypal Psychology. What I discovered was this:

Cultural diversity, a primary source of human conflict, is not really about religion, politics or social organization. It's not even about ethnicity or race. While these are all critical components, they are only symptoms and trigger points for a much deeper and older dynamic. Cultural diversity is, foremost, about differences in the ways people have lived on and related to the earth.

As vast as history has been, the discipline of cultural anthropology teaches us there have only been four basic types of cultures: 1) **foraging** (hunting and gathering), 2) **horticultural**, 3) **agrarian**, and 4) **industrial**. These four cultures are represented perfectly in the unique cultural diversity—Apache/Navajo, Pueblo, Hispanic, and Anglo—found in the state of New Mexico where I have spent most of my adult life.

The Maya and Hopi speak of these shifts in terms of *Worlds*, and according to them, the *Fifth World* is upon us. For the Hopi these earth changes were forecasted to begin in 2005 (think South Asian Tsunami, Hurricane Katrina). East Indian philosophy speaks of this era as the *Kali Yuga*, the Bible as an endtime, and many indigenous groups from the Americas have forecasted tremendous earth changes. Probably the most well known, via a series of social movements starting with the Harmonic Convergence (1987), is the Mayan calendar. It reveals that everything is coming to a head in the year 2012, a dramatic shifting of both consciousness and social structures.

What these prophecies point to is really a keen sense of the obvious. In terms of ecological and societal tension, the industrial world is bumping up against its own limitations. Something has to budge. As is the underlying theme behind the title of this work, apocalyptic doesn't simply mean the end of something. It, foremost, points to *rebirth*. Although these various teachings may seem romantic and vague, what they suggest is profound. Culturally and psychologically, we need to remember all that we have been.

Revelations

Two life-transforming revelations supported this exploration. One occurred when I moved back to the American Southwest in the late 1980s after the completion of a graduate degree in Cultural Anthropology. I was reading Frank Waters' groundbreaking work, *Book of the Hopi* (1963), a rare instance in which indigenous peoples shared their prophecies with an outsider. There it all was. While couched in mythological terms, Waters' telling of the story of the

Hopi myth of Five Worlds indicated these stories held a sophisticated understanding of historical time.

The boldface words in parentheses are mine, indicating the anthropological parallels in Hopi oral traditions. "In the First World they had lived with the animals (**foraging**). In the Second World, they had developed handicrafts, homes, and villages (**horticulture**). Now in the Third World they multiplied in such numbers and advanced so rapidly that they created big cities, countries, and a whole civilization (**agrarian**). This made it difficult for them to conform to the plan of Creation and to sing praises.... More and more of them became wholly occupied with their own earthly plans." The Fourth World (**industrial**) is then described as "where all the people went on their migrations to the ends of the earth and back," and "a full expression of man's ruthless materialism and imperialistic will." (Waters 1963) These prophecies, in other words, were the mythological way of recording history, an uncanny understanding of how cultural evolution has unfolded.

The foraging and horticultural cultures were fairly egalitarian, that is, no one had a whole lot of power over another. Together they will be referred to as *tribal*. Agrarian cultures introduced hierarchies; that is, societies composed of "haves and have-nots," which most often appeared as chiefdoms and feudalistic monarchies. The industrial world attempts to throw democracy, economic and spiritual free will into the mix, but hierarchies based on power and wealth remain entrenched. In the 21st century we are, more so than ever, a complex and often confusing mixture of these four types of cultures, or what will hereafter be referred to as Worlds.

As analyzed by the discipline of anthropology, the complementary layers of infrastructure, social structure, and superstructure hold each of these Worlds together. *Infrastructure* refers to economy, how a group feeds themselves and survives on the earth. *Social structure* is how society is organized (*i.e.*, marriage, education, government). *Superstructure* indicates how a people think, feel, and worship. Put all three together and you have the nuts and bolts of a culture.

Whereas the industrial World has threatened the survival of the infrastructures and social structures of earlier cultures, their superstructure, or what hereafter will simply be referred to as *consciousness*, doesn't change so easily. These differences in types of consciousness speak too much of the tension, both within us and in society, that the planet is experiencing. The prophecies are suggesting that these older ways of culture must be restored and balanced with the newer—a kind of cultural resurrection that must occur, foremost, from within.

Apocalyptic Grace is a disciplined, grounded understanding of these prophecies. It provides the evolutionary understanding that the wisdom traditions, from shamanism to the world religions, were well aware of the kinds of earth changes, internally and externally, that anthropologists and psychologists of the modern era have now been uncovering. What these older philosophies and modern social sciences have in common is tracking the evolving soul of humanity.

Revitalization

The second revelation central to this work occurred to me many moons ago while surveying the anthropology shelves in the Temple University library. At that time, I was an undergraduate Comparative Religion student, a mere teenager. I picked out the book, *Revitalization Movements* (1956) by Anthony F. C. Wallace, and I flashed upon the whole of time. By hook or by crook, culture will revitalize itself. Like life itself, culture's will to survive is irrepressible.

While most of the planet is doing this dance to an international monetary system and the demands of an industrial order, there are deep undercurrents in the psyche that recall older cultural ways of surviving. What then does a Fifth World have in store for us? Perhaps for the first time in the history of the planet, we can look back at our entire evolution, take our ethnocentric blinders off, and begin to fully understand and appreciate our differences. This is an unprecedented opportunity for the species.

For better and worse, again as the prophecies suggest, it may take shades of apocalypse (*i.e.,* worldwide economic collapse, the tragic intra-warfare of the Abrahamic faiths, ecologically induced disasters) to be able to receive this information. The psyche, in its movements to alleviate tension and resolve conflict, provides *numinous* (meaning filled with a sense of the presence of divinity, appealing to the higher emotions or to the aesthetic sense) experience. This is its inbuilt nature.

Through this experience, a new kind of anchoring opportunity is afforded to re-envision one's life and the world. When the power of numinous experience begins to work upon a collective body of people, therein we see the origins of religion and social movements. Anthropology calls this movement *Revitalization.*

When a people and a culture get their backs pushed up against the wall, when they are looking at the possibility of their own extinction, a *collective unconscious* envisioning process occurs that offers both a psychological and social way out. In the last century and a half, we have seen this rampant among both colonized peoples and colonizers who felt disenfranchised from their own cultures. The Ghost Dance, Peyote Religion, the Rastafarian movement, the Western fascination with, and the New Age are all examples of this.

This process, however, can quickly become co-opted and corrupted by the entrepreneurial tendencies of World Four. Prime examples are Rastafarian dreadlocks, colors and garb. This is a movement that began in the 1930s as a visionary, anti-imperialistic brand of Africanized Christianity that has since become mainstream chic.

Reggae, the Rastafarian synthesis of ritual and popular music, is now used as a kind of elevator music for "hip" establishments, while all the Rastafarian paraphernalia can be picked up at your local shopping mall or head shop. The symbolism remains, but its full potency has been bought off. This is how capitalism often survives. It doesn't defeat its opponents. It absorbs them. The Gods descend into the marketplace.

However, no matter the absorption rate, a new synthesis has occurred. Again using Rastafarians as an example, and however this movement has been mainstreamed, it has now joined the ranks of World Religions. Rastafari became a global movement by adding a potent pop culture ritual form and pronounced social agenda to a Christian belief system. Most importantly, social movements are parallel to the drive for revitalization within the psyche itself. Social liberation and the quest for personal liberation become simultaneous movements.

The Homestretch

Apocalyptic Grace boils down to this: Each of us is the world soul unfolding. The cross-pollination of Worlds the industrial era (World Four) has created an unprecedented global archetypal pool of information and activity. Disco is big in India, salsa and reggae in Japan, and Tibetan Buddhism is the fastest growing grassroots religious movement in the United States. No culture, no matter how traditional it appears, is untouched by this strange twist of events.

Whereas in the past, religious meaning and figures largely filled in the content of archetypal forms, nowadays style, artistic pursuits, recreational activities, and social movements, readily substitute for that same numinous experience. The common denominator, however, remains the same. As Buddhism put into doctrine, all human beings suffer and thus all human beings seek to resolve their predicament.

The silver lining is this. Suffering always contains an element of the transpersonal; that is, it goes beyond one's mundane self in a redemptive way. And for most of us, suffering is the doorway, the impetus, and the vehicle, into the transcendent. As seen throughout history and culture, if we can't go beyond ourselves, it is very difficult to live with ourselves.

These same principles of consciousness also apply for culture. World Four, the industrial order, is being confronted by its own ethnocentrism. On the other side of that limitation is the potential for an unprecedented planetary cultural sharing.

Archetypes: The Metaphoric Mind

The immediate challenge in describing the evolution of consciousness is that there is a metaphoric quality to consciousness that defies any straightforward scientific categorization. Indeed, metaphor seems to be at the origin and core of the human experience. Some 50,000 years ago, our ancestors began etching, drawing, and painting images on the sides of cliffs and caves. The impact of those images on the budding human psyche was as great or greater than reality itself. Such is the power of the archetype.

Derived from a Greek word and concept meaning "pattern," the eminent psychologist Carl Jung understood the archetype as a largely unconscious *energetic* that actually precedes any type of symbolic representation. In other words, we are and act out on our archetypes before we even have a chance to think about them. This is their allure as well as their danger. Archetypes are not particularly conscious.

Though animals also seem to apprehend the world through archetypes—they, too, go into a dream world—the human species was now capable of manufacturing such archetypes. Paleolithic drawings, created during a time period stretching from 50,000 to

10,000 BCE, show up all over the planet. The prevailing anthropological evidence suggests that as a species we migrated from Africa
into the Middle East and Central Asia. The oldest archeological set-
tlement seems to be in present-day Israel, some 100,000 years ago.
What was later to become the God of Abraham, Jacob and Isaac
was, traced back far enough over time, the common denominator
genetic pool that would link all of humanity.

From this central crossroads, humans fanned out to the north
and west, the European stock, and to the East, eventually crossing from Asia into the Americas via boat and/or a land-ice bridge.
While the genetic confirmation of all of this is still being explored,
what can be established is this: from Europe across Siberia to Native America, from Africa across the Middle East to India, and then
on to Eastern Asia the Pacific Islands and Australia, a global artistic
consciousness had arrived. These were the planet's first pictorial archetypes, which went hand-in-hand with depicting a long history
of deity figures. This was humanity's God gene.

In this way, archetypes are not simply symbolic reflections
of human reality, but become the lens by which humans come to
know reality. Though the term *archetype* is only used by a slim mar-
gin of the planet's population, all people use archetypes to *indi-
viduate*, that is, move through the dilemmas of their lives as though
they were heroes on a journey. And, in case this notion of archetype
already seems too abstract or spiritual, pick your favorite TV show,
novel, historical, religious, sports and/or popular culture figure,
and therein you will quickly find a connection to the prominent
archetypes operating within you.

Okay, still too abstract? Think of Tom Hanks in the Robin-
son Crusoe movie story, *Cast Away*. He painted a face onto a soccer
ball and called it Wilson. The ongoing dialogue he had with Wilson
kept him sane. When he lost Wilson on the seas, he felt true grief.
This is how it is with our archetypes. Without them, our imagina-
tions would have no one to talk to.

Toward the end of his life, Jung suggested that archetypes are more than just spiritual or symbolic notions. Archetypes are at the foundation of the thinking process, "an inherited mode of psychic functioning, corresponding to the inborn way in which the chick emerges from the egg, the bird builds its nest, a certain kind of wasp stings the motor ganglion of the caterpillar, and eels find their way to Bermuda" (Whitmont, *The Symbolic Quest*, 1969). Archetypes are how humans see and experience the world.

Curiously, it is conflict (and the various kinds of pain connected with it) and not harmony that, moreover, brings the awareness of how are archetypes are operating within us. Be it under emotional and/or physical stress, the core of our personalities, for better and worse, come out. How that conflict is dealt with, the quest for balance and resolution, forecasts where consciousness takes its next steps. Paradoxically, while archetypes are there to lead us out of our dilemmas, they may also pose them. Archetypes notoriously have both a light and dark side. The warrior can be a bully, the lover an addict, the caregiver a wounding martyr.

So it is as well with these four Worlds. While each of these Worlds has its own unique way of addressing and moving out of the dark, they, nevertheless, like individuals, are also capable of getting rather stuck. How we move out of that stuck-ness tells us what the *modus operandi*, the primary function, of a culture is. For tribal societies, this was the purpose of myth and ritual; for agrarian hierarchies, the disciplines of the world religions; for modern society, a similar purpose is being served by popular culture and psychology. The differences in the archetypal orientations of each of these Worlds are the underpinnings of cultural diversity. This is what this study is setting out to explore.

Cultural Diversity in a Nutshell

World One corresponds to the foraging phase, a period that consumed more than 90 percent of our time as a species. No matter who you currently are, if you dive deeply enough into your own heritage, this is where you will land. Men tended to tune out, to focus in, and to hunt. They couldn't do two things at a time. Still can't. Women came together, gathered, and tended to communicate. Sound familiar? Much of this foraging activity is literally built into our physiology, *i.e.*, the left brain/right brain differential between men and women corresponding to the demands of hunting versus gathering. Men tend to think in a more focused linear fashion. As hunters, they had to. Women, as gatherers and communicators, became much more capable of seeing the whole picture.

World One was the earnest attempt of a species now "sprung" from nature, but yet so inseparably tied into her cycles, to come to terms with the expansion of its own consciousness. There would be much in our humanity that could not escape the "flight or fight " messages that nature, as a safety and defense mechanism, brings to the nervous systems (systems that are ready to be nervous) of all of its living beings. As civilized as humanity would like to think it has become, it is our animal core, for better and worse, that brings us crashing back to our origins.

Our continual propensity for fear and violence paired with incredible potential for loving demonstrates this perplexing truth. We see this same paradox in the animal world. One moment a cat can be the softest, most loving creature curled up on your lap, and the next they are ready to torture, literally, another animal to its death. This element of paradox, what Jung called the **tension of the opposites**, would enter into all realms of the human experience. Jung's definition of maturity was the ability to hold two contradictory emotions at the same time.

An unending parade of polarities—life/death, love/hate, good/evil, celebration/grief, bliss/rage—could either provide the tension to frustrate and defeat us, or the challenge and incentive to transcend to more expanded states of consciousness. The choice was awkwardly ours. This is the emotional and spiritual arena that makes us humans human. It first comes to light in World One, but never goes away.

The core World One response was healing ceremonies utilizing the ancient cultural tools of myth and ritual. These societies were small scale and nomadic; if any one person's problems became too big, it would tear away at the whole social fabric. As they are not locked in to a particular schedule, other than a tracking of the herds, a ceremony can be called at any time to address the imbalances. The individual is ritually plugged into the figures of the pool of myths adapting to the needs of the individual. Conformity was the order of the day.

The science that horticultural society introduces is a more formal alignment of human society and structures with nature's geographic forms. Today this is called *geomancy*, or in the Oriental rendition, *Feng Shui*. Whereas the science of the foragers was, foremost, based on knowledge of animals, plants and herbology, here the attention shifted more to sacred sites and the skies, so as to afford an astronomical alignment of village structures and ceremony.

World Two also introduces an accompanying shift in consciousness. Attention is not simply focused on the archetypes of nature, but also the emergence of cultural heroes. Whereas the elemental forces of nature are still elicited, these forces also become more anthropomorphized within deity figures; that is, they begin to resemble us humans. There is an increasing emergence of Gods, and in particular Goddesses, as these cultures have a significant matriarchal bent with their cultivating attention to Mother Earth. The pantheons of the world's great bodies of mythologies (Greek,

Hindu, Roman, Celtic, Chinese, Egyptian, Mayan, etc.) all have their roots in World Two.

In contrast to the stereotype of the peaceful farmer, the most dramatic rise in the rate of warfare and disease occurs with this human domestication of nature. Now obliged to stay in one place to till the fields, the notion of territory became aligned with the notion of boundary. One piece of farmland becomes more choice than another. Such is the escalation of human oppression. The increased size and complexity instigated by village life marked the beginning of intra-tribal (within the tribe) and pan-tribal (several tribes) governing groups. These became precursors to the power wielding institutions of World Three. The once loosely organized priestly group evolved into a fixed ruling caste.

Here is the picture: World Three is about to arrive. Inevitably, many of these small-scale horticultural and relatively egalitarian societies evolved into agrarian cultures with entrenched hierarchies. Certain people have significant power and resources over others. The oldest indications of this shift occur in the congregation of peoples in the great river valleys of the world. Along the Nile River in Egypt, the Tigris and Euphrates Rivers in Mesopotamia (five to six thousand years BCE), and then along the Indus River in southern Asia and Yellow River valley in northern China (two to three thousand years BCE), a societal shift occurs that sets precedent for another revolution to hit the entire planet. With the exception of Australia, no continent, no race, would avoid this.

The Greek city-states, African monarchies, Native American empires, European (Vikings, Celtic, Roman) hierarchies, all would follow suit. Cultures, around the world, became caste structured, producing a perennial tension between the haves and have-nots, the dominant and the dominated. This would profoundly alter the psychology of the species.

In short, in World Three, the tribal world had gone amuck. The tribe could no longer provide the cohesion and healing that focused ritual provides. Its spirituality could be used as weaponry, with other tribes, within the tribe. This is what the Old Testament refers to as witchcraft. A new kind of suffering had arrived. People's welfare and well-being were falling through society's cracks. People could become alienated from their own societies, leading to a kind of *aloneness* that would, at once, give rise to what psychology calls the ego, and an appeal for a resolution to the dilemma of the ego. There wasn't just the suffering of the human condition, but the increasing suffering of how one might be treated by one's own culture.

The evolving religions of World Three sought to repair the very alienation this new type of culture was creating. Polytheistic religions became hierarchal, reflecting the stratified social structure. At the top of this pyramid was the king whose decisions, in theory, would represent a kind of divine connection with the Gods. In Middle Eastern culture, this gaze upwards would eventually point to a One God, a monotheistic emphasis (Zoroastrianism, Judaism, Christianity, Islam) that would impact, if not take over, most of the world. The Eastern world religions (Jainism, Hinduism, Buddhism) were more monistic in outlook, with an emphasis on the Oneness of all things, but a similar function was being served. These were all umbrella belief systems that were created to span the differences and resolve the tensions that the breakdown of the tribal world was creating.

Coinciding with the spiritual dissolution of these tribal worlds were the rise of hierarchal regimes (chiefdoms, nobilities) that fail to accommodate the spiritual needs of a growing, oppressed underclass. While each of these religions would have their particular tangents, their underlying response was nearly identical: ethical imperatives and spiritual disciplines addressing the problem of suffering. The notable difference between East and West was that the Eastern religions were much more tolerant and absorbing of their shamanic and polytheistic roots. The internal shift, however, was again similar—a movement into centralized deities, figures and notions—Moksha, Yahweh, Buddha, Nirvana, Samadhi, Christ, Allah—that condensed and refined the archetypal journey in a world becoming all too complex and unjust.

Much has been made out of the difference between East and West, but their societal impetus was fairly alike: a reaching out for a redemption beyond societal hardship and injustice which these new religions—Judaism, Christianity, Islam, Hinduism, Buddhism—promised and tried to provide. **Inevitably, these religions became a part of the very hierarchies they were originally critiquing**. Religion itself became a complex affair, on the one hand providing hope and redemption for the disenfranchised, on the other becoming equally capable of perpetuating and enforcing the injustices of hierarchy.

Eventually, the constraints of this hierarchal World would be the primary impetus for the emergence of World Four, a way out of the stranglehold of dictatorial and theocratic regimes. While many of the injustices of World Three continued in a class-entrenched capitalist society, there were new freedoms won as well, leading to an entirely new psychology. For better and worse, the experience and notion of *self* became ever more pronounced.

Liberation from slavery and racial, gender, and ethnic inequalities were laced into the ideals of World Four, but it would take centuries for that liberation to truly unfold. Democracy becomes the *modus operandi* of World Four, although we see plenty of examples of it in Worlds One and Two. Its maturation and fruition still seem to await us. Instead, we begin to be ruled by oligarchies, many of them "behind the scenes" groups, now tied into the demands of a world economic system.

Individuation, once the cornerstone of World One's central vision quest ritual, returns in a whole new fashion. Capitalism becomes the modern's (sometimes all too aggressive) vision quest. The mechanistic worldview, a product of the scientific revolution, reinforces this quest. The untold story, which the chapter on World

Four will address, is that the modern, scientific world-view was not, as generally depicted, the rise of "Reason" from the medieval depths of faith and superstition. It was, instead, the outcome of an ideological warfare between the growing polarities of Renaissance Europe: urban vs. rural, Christian vs. pagan, Neoplatonic vs. Aristotelian, Inquisitional vs. Alchemical, that brought the European continent to its knees. And, of course, amidst all of this, was the Reformation's splintering off from the Catholic Church into all kinds of other dissenting sects that all had a very hard time getting along with each other.

When the dust settled, the fruit of the scientific revolution, the experimental method, was separated from its own cultural foundations (Neoplatonism, Hermeticism, Alchemy). In short, the *mental* perspective was born at the expense of its metaphysical roots. The Inquisition made any kind of *archetypal exploration* outside of the confines of the Church perilous. While the Reformation was responding to the Church's institutional corruption, much of its resulting institutions also perpetuated the accusations and persecutions of the Inquisition.

In brief, the Inquisition was the European conflict between the central hierarchal power of World Three, the Church, and older World Two rural village communities and an influx of ancient Greek, Egyptian and Arabic wisdom traditions. Eventually, the mechanistic paradigm, the Universe and human body as machine, aims to resolve this tension. Abnormal and eccentric mental behavior were seen as no longer signs of the Devil, but as *psychopathologies* the new paradigm of psychology was setting out to explore and categorize. Meanwhile, the new Science synthesized and advanced upon these wisdom traditions, but their broader philosophical and spiritual foundations were cut away. God goes into hiding.

Communitas—Promises of a Fifth World

Ironically, the psychological therapies prescribed for the industrialized age are not substantially different from the soul retrievals and redemptive spiritual paths forged in the earlier Worlds. Pieces of our psyche have been torn asunder, cast away, forgotten, and the quest is to recoup wholeness. Similarly, much of the principles and cathartic practices embedded within the rituals and myths of the indigenous cultures, and later with the emergence of the world religions, now also show up in the arts, entertainment, sporting events, political spectacles, and media onslaught of popular culture. While much of the modern's impulse becomes secularized and commercialized, the same cultural, psychological and spiritual functions are still being served.

This is what the late anthropologist Victor Turner (*The Ritual Process*, 1969) called the drive for *communitas*, a notion that will be used as a conceptual thread to link all of these Worlds. Communitas is the impulse to transcend the constraints of our human condition into greater states of communion. Communitas generally refers to the physiological and psychological benefits of ritual energy, but it can also be achieved in the potency and privacy of one's own meditation, prayer, and/or recreational life. It can also come about through the simple modern urge "to party the night away."

With the increasing loss of community ritual and family structure for the modern, the unmet need for communitas has also sown the seeds of his/her addictions. The origins of many of today's more severe addictions—alcohol, cocaine, opiates—can be found in late 19th century Western culture, a time in which a secularized mindset was inundating the Western psyche. Men and women were equally prone. If the culture would not give us a vital and consistent communitas experience, then drugs would fill in the gap. In that same light, it is no wonder the 20th century would rebound with all kinds of resurrected mysticisms and New Age aspirations.

Family Life

Industrialization leads to a dissolution of the extended family structure of the earlier agrarian Worlds. As most of the planet would eventually become, more or less, industrialized, this would begin to infect the social structure of these other Worlds as well. The extended family gets whittled back down to the nuclear family structure, which, by the second half of the 20th century, itself begins to break down. In the United States, at the dawning of the 21st century, approximately only 25 percent of the nuclear families remain intact. The "dysfunctional family" became the norm.

And yet, individually and culturally, it is stunning that we are as functional we are. What culture takes away on the one hand, it compensates for on the other. The language and melding of psychology, self-help popular culture, and New Age spiritualities become a new norm. And, there is a return, often evangelical, to tried-and-true religion. Religious improvisation and fundamentalism grow side by side. Either way, the wisdom of ancient worlds is being dipped back into.

This is the point. Evolution is not just out there. Evolution is, foremost, within us. And while evolution rarely goes backwards, it can also never forget. And, as is taught in basic anthropology, the most daunting challenge of being human is stepping outside of one's own ethnocentrism, of one's own cultural paradigm. The world is the way it is because that is how we've been taught to see it. However, the modern psyche, perhaps more so than ever, is groping for wholeness, and, lo and behold, a wholeness that can only come about, as is this book's persistent theme, through an integration of all that we have been; a wholeness that comes about through our willingness to cross back and forth between Worlds.

Passage between Worlds

Within the dawning ranks of psychology, Carl Jung courageously chose to go on a journey, both across s and back through time. He went straight from his tutelage with Freud to working with indigenous peoples in North America, Africa and India, as well as diving back into Europe's alchemical, Gnostic, and Hermetic spiritual past. Jung understood that the healing of the psyche went hand in hand with an understanding and healing of history. The integration of dream, archetypal forces, ritual and myth, divinely experienced in previous eras, must now be sought within the particular dynamics of the modern's psyche and activities. Attempting to balance all of these different Worlds, both inner and outer, the patient must make that passage across these vast differences. The patient must become his own modern day *shaman*.

In terms of evolutionary time, we, as a species, are experiencing a profound mid-life crisis. Our ways of being—the evolution of the shamanic, ancient and modern mind sets—correspond with our ways of living on the earth (the tribal, agrarian, and industrial). That evolution is now crying out for recognition and synthesis. It seems that our current dysfunctions may galvanize this next leap of consciousness. We are now, as Native prophecies have suggested, perched on the edge of the next World. The way that will unfold is not yet entirely known.

I hesitate to use the word prophecies for two reasons. There is a political charge around it in that it may be inappropriate and/or politically incorrect for a non-Native to be talking of these prophecies. The second is that what is being called "prophecies" is really a basic sense of history and the major shifts our evolution as a species have taken us through. As a student of culture and spirituality, my interest, then, is not concentrated in the prophecies themselves, but the underlying shifts they are pointing to.

Much of the world's scriptures (the *Bible, Bhagavad-Gita, Qur'an, Vedas, Upanishads*) can be understood in the same way. They are largely focused on the transitions of the tribal Worlds One and Two to a stratified one (World Three). The Judeo-Christian lineage does speak of an *endtime*; indeed, it posits personal salvation as the solution to this dilemma of time. The more Pentecostal interpretation speaks of this in terms of the "Rapture," which for some justifies what can be construed as the "holy wars" now threatening the planet. The Hopi prophecy speaks of a similar endtime, of two world wars and perhaps a third, but it holds out as well for other redemptive possibilities.

Some of them, of course, retained the wisdom granted them upon their Emergence. With this wisdom they understood that the farther they proceeded on the Road of Life and the more they developed, the harder it was. That was why their world was destroyed every so often to give them a fresh start (Waters 1963).

While apocalyptic like the Bible, the evolutionary understanding of Hopi prophecy is that only in becoming fully conscious of what we are dying to can we fully embody what we are being reborn to. Such is the parallel nature of the psychological process as well. Inner work crosses all boundaries of time and space.

And so is the nature of the fall of World Four, now embodied in a teetering world economy. The dying has already pointed to rebirth. World Five is not coming. It is already here. It is showing up in the increasing multicultural spread of both our communities and inner life. It is showing up in our abilities to revitalize and link what was essential about each of these previous Worlds: 1) the hero's journey, 2) local and regional sustainability, 3) the powers of living an obedient, prayerful life, 4) the opportunities of choice. The fall of World Four is allowing the possibilities of World Five to fully emerge.

Structure

The next five chapters, each devoted to the archetypal perspectives and implications of the Five Worlds, will be sweeping through history and culture with broad and grand generalizations. In no way does this accurately describe the tremendous variety of nuance within those cultures. Instead, the objective is to uncover the major evolutionary trends as cultures move from World One through World Four, and engage the prospects of World Five.

It is to be understood that for every instance cited of a specific cultural trait characteristic of a certain World, there are no doubt other cultures with opposite or different traits. The point, again, is to simply note the general direction the evolutionary trend is heading, and how this ends up in qualitative differences between the different Worlds. It is also to be understood that each World grows from the seeds of the previous World. Thus, to discuss any particular World invites a discussion of its connection to all of the Worlds.

The first four chapters on the Worlds are broken down into four sections each. The first, Global Archetypal Unfolding, will assess the broad themes, principles, and practices of each World as it encircles the planet. The second section, Cultures of the Southwest, utilizes the special occurrence that the spread of cultures in the American Southwest—the Athabaskan, the Pueblo, the Old World Hispanic, the Anglo—and how they respectively represent the Four Worlds. The third section, Personal Journey, anchors this understanding of cultural diversity by deciphering the contents of individual consciousness—in this case my own.

The fourth section, Practical Applications, provides a hands-on brass tacks survey of working with these different Worlds. I present case studies of my clients and students that indicate how to elicit and discern the general principles of each of these Worlds as they operate in any given individual. This combination of global, local, and personal archetypal unfolding allows us to cross-reference and interpret any cultural dynamic by linking its external history with the awareness of our own inner cultural diversity.

At times, particularly as I introduce each new World, the writing takes liberties with verb tenses and metaphors. World One is written mostly in past tense, as this is the 90 percent of our time as a species, "the ever-present origin" (Gebser 1986) out from which the rest of the human story unfolds. But then, with each subsequent World, the image I'm hoping to capture is that we are on a journey across time, both within and outside of ourselves. The feeling is that as we are perched on the quest of understanding history and culture, we are witness in present time to how this journey is layered within us. Just as the Hopi language structure has no clearly demarcated past and future tense—everything is connected to the unfolding of the present—*Apocalyptic Grace* tries to describe these Worlds like we are *present* at the time of their emergence. In the reality of the psyche, we are. The past slips into the present and beckons the future. In other words, bear with what may seem at times unconventional English, or for some, simply bad grammar.

The Purpose

No matter what our culture of origin, we all face the challenge of integrating all of these Worlds and breaking through to World Five. The final chapter, "Coming of Age in a World without Borders," looks at those possibilities. My motivations are this: We have become a multicultural world characterized and plagued by racial, ethnic, religious, socioeconomic, and political differences and tensions. While the ground floor of most psychological methodologies may begin with establishing emotional balance alongside healthy intimate and social relationships, cultural dynamics are inseparably tied into to how this all unfolds. So, whether it is in working out one's own stuff, addressing tensions in our communities, or resolving international political conflict, what is being asked of us is an integration of consciousness.

What brings these two arenas, the psychological and the cultural, together, is what the founders of psychology called the *collective unconscious*, or the earlier forays into spirituality referred to as the *soul*. To stay, from a psychological perspective, in just the arena of resolving dysfunction, or, in the cultural arena, on the subjects of race, religion, socioeconomics, and politics, is to miss out on an invitation into their deeper connection.

All that has been with us is still with us. All that has been with us may be picked up and tried again. There is the inevitable risk of dilution and forgery, the quick fix spiritual and psychological supermarket techniques, we are bombarded with. There is, fortunately, wisdom to be found in those supermarkets as well. And, there is, at the same time, the unprecedented surfacing and sharing of information and the globe's esoteric traditions. This grand mix is what World Five is about.

Beneath the dazzling kaleidoscope of information, universal principles—catharsis, balance, attunement, restoration, and compassion—still seem to abide. Our rudder is the contours of the soul, that membrane that connects our inner turbulence, passions, and peace with all of the contents and issues of the world, both past and present. Our rudder is the ever changing intermingling of archetypes that puts into one basket the fruits of all of the Worlds.

Nearly twenty years ago I had this dream. I was picking up the receiver from a telephone booth where a huge elk, in riding upon his shoulders, had deposited me in the sacred foothills of the Taos Pueblo. A voice, calling himself God, on the other end of that telephone line had informed me that "the soul is an elusive partnership." The purpose and mission of *Apocalyptic Grace* is to make that partnership less elusive, to track the ancient archetypal energies we are still dancing with. And to dance that dance within the cutting-edge flair of the present.

Summary

This introduction provides an overview by which to track the purpose and entire journey of *Apocalyptic Grace*. The discipline of Cultural Anthropology is reiterating what Native prophecies, most notably the Hopi and Mayan, have long known. As a species we have gone through distinct stages of cultural evolution, known as Worlds, and we are now bumping up against the possibilities of the next (Fifth) World. The Jungian notion of archetype helps us track, within the psyche, the differences in these Worlds. Because of the psyche's inherent move toward wholeness, there is now unprecedented opportunity to integrate those differences to become truly global, multicultural citizens.

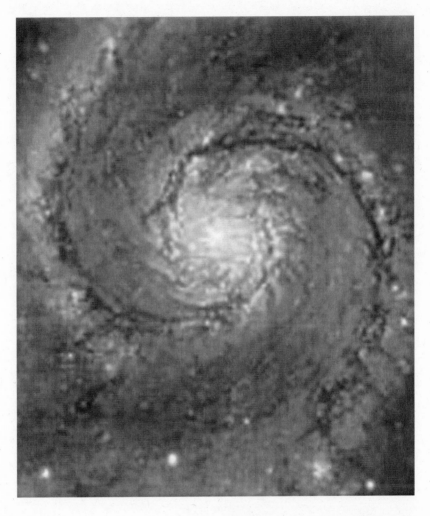

SHAMANISM

WORLD ONE
The Magic of It All

MIND
Air

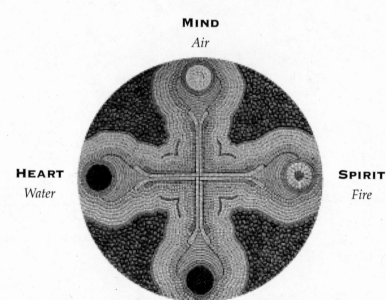

HEART
Water

SPIRIT
Fire

BODY
Earth

First Onset:

50,000 BCE — 10,000 BCE

Predominant Infrastructure:

HUNTING AND GATHERING

Predominant Social Structure:

BAND, NUCLEAR FAMILY

Predominant Superstructure:

SHAMANISM

Predominant Medicinal Response:

HERBOLOGY / PURIFICATION, RESTORATION

Predominant Mode of Thinking:

SHAMANIC

Human Potential Advance:

EGALITARIAN SOCIAL ORDER, MEDICINE WHEEL PSYCHOLOGY

Shadow Sides:

OVER-IDENTIFICATION WITH MYTHOLOGICAL FIGURES, LACK OF CONSCIOUS AWARENESS

American Southwest Culture:

ATHABASKAN (NAVAJO / APACHE)

Personal Journey:

PEYOTE MEDICINE, VISION QUEST, TRANCE POSSESSION

Global Archetypal Unfolding
The Art of the Matter

There is no definitive date of origin to this journey. There are, however, plenty of clues strewn along the way. Some two million years ago, our ancestors began to hunt. The mystical solidarity that the hunters developed with their prey would play a major part in the birthing of human consciousness. The next major shift, some 500,000 years later, arrived when males began to identify themselves as fathers. This new branch in the primate family grew completely apart from the rest of the tree.

An extra kind of socializing process arrived. The "father" phenomenon, combined with the biological shift that the human female became sexually available most times of the month, rather than periods of going into heat, allowed for a democratizing of the pecking order. Thus, the less "alpha" males were more apt to find partners. A novel kind of consciousness, a couple's consciousness, hit the planet. Mom and Dad acknowledged that they both had to raise a child.

The first documented use of fire occurs about 600,000 BCE, and with that an evolving mastery of the natural elements—earth, wind, water, and fire. Making all kinds of weapons and tools accelerated the mission. Technology was always a part of the human story. This scrawny, fairly hairless ape became capable of surviving in nearly every ecosystem on the planet.

The artwork that showed up in the late Paleolithic, some 50,000 years ago, created the most significant leap in the foundation of the human psyche. Imaginative realities, that had long been part of the psyche of much of the animal world, were now being etched into and portrayed on the sides of rock walls and caves around the world. Whereas animals have also been nocturnal dreamers, subject to the impulses and imagery of their own unconscious, the human drive to depict those realities changed our relationship to its contents. The ability to depict an image that was not "real" but often had more power over us than if it were real, was humanity's launching pad. Such is the power and presence of the archetype.

The first pictorial archetypes were aboard the planet. "The hunter of the good heart" (Cajete, *Native Science*, 2000), the mixture of human and animal bodies, were the most pervasive. They indicated the dramatic communion of spirit and blood that the killing of another species for survival invoked. An ecological ethic was at work here. The reverence for life, even amidst the taking of life, was upheld.

Another core archetype was also showing up, one that put the human species in touch with a healing process that equally became aligned with the origins of religion. The snake, the power of the serpent, was beginning to uncoil. This power was elaborately described and worked with in the East Indian yogic/shamanic disciplines as *kundalini,* in the Western ancient healing traditions of Asceplius as *Cadeuces,* and in the respective Aztec, Maya and Pueblo traditions as *Quetzalcoatl, Kulkulkan,* and *Avanyu.*

The snake represented what Sigmund Freud would later call the *id* or basic instincts. But, as colored by the scientific paradigm of World Four, Freud would rationalize the exalted connection. Without a "higher force" tempering the snake, then culture doesn't stand a chance. Left unchecked, the id's domain, sex and hunger, turn into lust and greed. We're back to being baboons in the bush. Might makes right.

Profoundly, World One went deliberately across the grain of our primate origins. It was egalitarian. No one had substantial power over anyone else. Thus, there was the need for shaman-based ritual to invoke a more exalted energy to ensure both this social and psychological order. Among Native American cultures, the Eagle has always represented that higher force.

There is old film footage, shot in the early 1900s, of Hopi dancers in front of Washington, D.C. federal buildings reaching down into baskets of rattlesnakes. The dancers then dance freely with the snakes in their mouths. Next to them are other dancers fluttering Eagle feathers towards those snakes. With the dancers invoking the presence of the Eagle, the snakes don't dare rebel.

Tracking how this serpent energy moves in the body was what kundalini yoga practitioners, a shamanic cultural core to East Indian tribes, made into a science. Chakras, meaning "spinning disk," represent the different energy centers of the body. They have corresponding psychological and physical attributes that they refer to. The serpent energy begins in the sacrum region, the base chakra, released up through the spine, the other chakras, and then finally towards and out through the top of the head. The accompanying transformation is from raw, survival needs to the expansion of the heart and spiritual vision.

The Hopi spoke of this event as the *Emergence*, which was experienced also through the crown chakra or energy center, or what they called the "kopavi." In Native American cultures, the Eagle represented this crown chakra awareness. A later religion depicted this as a halo over the head of its savior, Jesus the Christ.

In much of African culture, this rise of kundalini was induced by vigorous rhythm, song and dance, and could be much more swift. A trance possession state may occur in which the individual momentarily lost consciousness. Overall, a common cross-cultural theme emerged. A physical, emotional, mental and spiritual clearing was called for and received. A kind of divine awareness arrives that could be thought of as an "ever present origin" (Gebser 1986) for the species. Such awareness seemed to be at the foundation of all kinds of spiritual and exalted psychological experience to come.

The modern, no matter how clouded, still has access to this opening. And it is still the sacred technologies of sound, breath, rhythm and movement, as developed in World One, that most often transport humans to that opening. Indeed, many of the mechanisms of popular culture attempt to create what was once a more tribally cohesive state of affairs. All kinds of tribal behaviors still show up in the modern world (concerts, sporting events, religious services, meditation), although how this happens must now be sought within the choices of the individual. None of this penchant for catharsis, however, goes away.

"...da Original Funk..."

The origins of the word *funky* are West African. It was used to describe that "funky" smell when the song and dance of ritual were heating up. It has since become a popular culture term referring to a rhythmically "thick" soul sound coming out of African-American communities. Hunters and gatherers were the first funksters. They were the planet's first party animals.

An array of physically demanding techniques and rituals spurred on ecstatic music and dance. Humanity's first musical instruments, the voice and the drum, became our first party toys. These techniques of trance and ecstasy would be refined in an assortment of polytheistic rituals that would make up the East Indian practices of what came to be known as , and, in the Hellenistic world, a vast array of mystery cults. Shiva and Dionysus would become philosophical, if not historically linked, consorts (Danielou, *Shiva and Dionysus*, 1984).

The !Kung in Africa described these accelerated vibrations as boiling energy. It is this same phenomenon that later gets passed down to African-American communities through the medium of gospel music and dance. This was termed "getting happy." In World One, spirit possession was the order of the day. In World One, addiction and/or adverse effects were not much of an issue. "Partying down" was done in a ritually regulated manner. Today's party techniques are much more hit and miss. With the possibility, over the course of a lifetime, of substance abuse, it is no wonder that those in recovery, or the more quietly inclined, turn to more sober spiritual exercises such as meditation and prayer. But let's not throw the baby out with the bathwater. Catharsis, the need for release, is bred into our DNA.

Bradford Keeney has made it his life journey to master and teach this type of healing, as fully embodied in his last work, *Shaking Medicine: The Healing Power of Ecstatic Movement* (2007). Ecstasy, derived from the Greek *ecstasis*, means to stand outside one's self. As Keeney explains,

> The most powerful form of healing and well-being comes when both hyperarousal and deep relation are cycled together, one taking place in relationship to the other. When we shake ourselves to the fullest height of ecstatic expression and then fall into the deepest state of quiet, we set the stage for powerful realignment and evolution of our whole being. This is the whole pattern of holistic medicine.

Keeney then unravels the evolutionary ride this special type of healing takes.

> In China the name for this hypothesized energy is *chi* or *qi*. It is called *ki* in Japan, *n/om* among the Kalahari Bushmen, *tumpinyeri mooroop* among some Aboriginal Australians, prana in India, *yesod* by Jewish kabbalists, Holy Spirit by Christians, *baraka* by Sufis, *manitou* by the Ojibway, and *ha* in Hawaii. Among many indigenous people it is simply referred to as *medicine*.

The healing power of World One would pervade the core of the Worlds to come.

The major human potential advance within the cultures of World One came down to this. As ancestral primates, the intensities of the psyche were once simply played out in nature's instinctual patterns of dominance and physical and sexual release. In World One, those intensities must be removed from the social arena or that arena would be quickly destroyed. Whether over a health, emotional, spiritual, or livelihood issue, if the tensions of any one individual became too great, it threatened the solidarity and effectiveness of the entire group. The community needed a healing. A ceremony was called.

Since hunters and gathers were small and flexible nomadic clans, this was easily accomplished. These breaks with the profane, foremost, served to siphon off the tensions of societal and psychological pressures. These tensions, instead, were played out in sacred ritual dramas. The mythological figures helped absorb the blows the individual could not in real life. These archetypes have experienced and worked through, in eternity, the daily trials that challenge us mere humans. This mythic scenario would remain with us throughout all of the subsequent Worlds.

By heroically plugging ourselves into the symbolic journeys of these eternal figures, humans are able to ritually embody and work through the drama of their own lives. We become the hero or the heroine. Like the figures in the myth we become identified with, our intent is to return again triumphant and healed. Absolutely pivotal is the creating of a regenerative energy in which the well being of the individual and group are restored.

The crucial ingredient in World One was that sacred time and space were fairly open-ended. The ritual, generally speaking, continued until the job got done. This could last days. With each succeeding World, ritual gets more controlled and limited by the demands of religious institutions. Conformity is on the rise. The secularization of World Four, the modern age, attempts to break out of this box. Much of this mythic scenario plays itself out in what individuals do with their own psychological and recreational outlets.

Through the ecstasis that the rituals of World One were designed to induce, a kind of grace, an abiding peace, is introduced. This comes about through a full participatory identification with the archetypes that are being invoked. It is this peace that the later ascendance of the world religions, with a variety of techniques and scripture, would equally attempt to cultivate. The question remains whether the power of this identification with archetypal figures has become increasingly lost to us? And how conscious were we about all of this in the first place? Is spirituality just a culturally enforced hypnosis, or is there true transcendence in the mix?

Tracking the World:
What a Tele-Pathetic Situation

This much we know. For some 25,000 years, for some 15,000 years before the advent of agriculture, hunting and gathering cultures were recording, analyzing, memorizing, and using for practical purposes, information about the lunar and solar cycles. Although World Two later developed more elaborate calendar systems with the Neolithic Revolution, World One produced the first astronomers. Combined with the knowledge of herbology, these were also the first scientists and physicians.

The irony is that for generations the modern thought of the indigenous people of this planet as rudimentary and simplistic. Their way of interacting with the cosmos was thought of as fanciful and superstitious. They acted, in other words, much like children. I will suggest that this, in fact, is the case, but in their childlike nature is the power of this World.

The belief that all of the natural world (plant, animal, and stone) have soul qualities like humans, that disasters occur because the wind or the clouds or the earth are mad at us, is an example of this childish nature. But it is precisely this soul quality and perception that serves as the *modus operandi* by which many an indigenous culture has survived. It begins with the notion (as does many an indigenous ceremony) that we are all related.

Everything—every thought, every action—affects everything else. Nothing escapes the web of life. The biological implications of this have been born out by scientists studying and confirming that the earth is one seething, interconnected Gaian organism (Lovelock,

The Ages of Gaia, 2000). The key factor to this awareness, as is the foundation of most organized ceremony, is the spirit of devotion.

Why this all works, or has the potential to work, is because the core of the unconscious is not just perpetual imagination or fantasy, but rather telepathy. We are not just hanging out here in the Universe. The Universe, quite the alive place, is also hanging out in us. The Universe, through all kinds of animals and natural forces, speaks to us. We can speak back to the Universe. Anthropology has called this *animism*. The shaman becomes adept at meaningfully passing back and forth between worlds. So does the depth psychologist. The shaman calls this matrix the spirit world, the psychologist, the collective unconscious.

Dying to One's Self

The primary difference for the modern versus the indigenous mind is that how the unconscious used to "play itself out" via myth and ritual has now become fragmented and much more of a private affair. We must now plummet the depth of our own psyches to discover the patterns that define our own unique story. Despite the fragmentation, there are some universal "hitching posts," principles that seem universal. Foremost is the premise that the Jungian notion of individuation, the maturation of self, does not correspond with the modern notion of individuality. To the contrary, individuation is about contacting the depths we humans have in common, a necessary series of deaths and rebirth.

The mother and father are first to die. In indigenous puberty ritual, the propelling force of a culture, the "emotional cords" with the parents are cut. The shadow sides of the mother archetype (any emotional and instinctual dynamic that has a person in its grip) and the shadow sides of the father archetype (coercive societal values that have overstepped the "natural laws" of the universe) are increasingly released. Deeper, healthier facets of the mother/father archetypes are to be attained.

In Chinese culture, this was known as the dynamic of *yin* and *yang*, and, in much of Native American culture, as *mother earth* and *father sky*. Mom and Dad could never crack how to be who they were supposed to be—foremost, the child's idealized image of them. A deeper, culturally generated grounding in the feminine and masculine must be sought.

However, it is not some facile harmony that is found here. It is, rather, a unifying process inherently bred on conflict (sometimes brutal), a tension (sometimes paralyzing) of the opposites. Like my cute little cat, at one instant we are absolutely darling little creatures, the next we are prepared to pounce and, if need be, kill. The tougher sides of the masculine (*i.e.*, the raging warrior) and the feminine (*i.e.*, the devouring mother) must be worked through. This is the imagery and energy that ancient ritual presents. It is the culture's job to prepare the initiate to be able to get through this. In working through this tension, a breakthrough occurs. This is what Jung called "the transcendent function."

Animism, also labeled in anthropology as "Participation Mystique" (Levy-Bruhl, *How Natives Think*, 1926), is the foundational awareness of World One. Much of modern psychology speaks of this state as a regression, a submission to "The Great Mother" (Newmann 1972), meaning a fairly unconscious state. (It makes sense the submission is to the Mother, as these were predominantly matriarchal cultures.) People were performing these rituals, but like worker bees submissive to their Queen, not real conscious about it.

The ability to effectively operate within these animistic rituals suggests to the contrary. To characterize a whole slice of culture as subsumed by the Great Mother (which is how the theorist Ken Wilber, 1996, generally thinks of indigenous culture), that is, the "unconscious," misses the vast complexity in archetypal and empirical mastery (*i.e.*, herbology, medically-proven forms of purification, the original calendars) these original foraging cultures brought upon the planet. This could not have been done in an unconscious state. These were not unconscious slouches.

Regression, being overwhelmed by the unconscious, is what indigenous cultures ritually attempt to overcome in the quest for balance and restoration. For the individual, this is the attempt of the hero to get out from under the sway of one's own psyche. On a personal level, regression can result in a complete breakdown. On a group level, regression leads to ritual abuse, as we've seen in forms of sacrifice, mass submission and killing. The ability to withstand this regression, to get to the transcendence waiting on the other side, mirrors the state of health in both the individual and the group. This, then, begs the question, what do we mean by health? To answer that, we must turn to humanity's first healers, the shaman.

Psychoneuroimmunology

The word *shaman* is actually of Siberian origin meaning "to see." Anthropologists noted that shamanism is a profession and a process in foraging cultures around the planet. The shaman was usually someone very good at and called to do what everyone had the inherent potential to do: the ability to see more deeply and help resolve the tendency for humans to throw themselves out of balance.

A modern medical term that explains the purpose of the shaman is *psychoneuroimmunology*. Breaking the word down into its parts, psycho-neuro-immune-ology refers to the study of the effect of the psyche (meaning soul in its original Greek) on the neurological system, and in turn, the impact on the immune system. Shamanic culture constitutes a cultivated grab bag of healing techniques with psychoneuroimmunological approaches (visualization, hypnosis, journeying, ritual process, and transformation) now being used in modern psychology. There is not a whole lot new under the sun. None of this could be achieved without invoking some form of a myth.

Whereas mythology might be thought of as merely a story, in the context of the psyche, myth is a way of seeing and apprehending the world. When embodied in ritual, the purpose of myth, as the partner to ritual, is also to redirect tension off of everyday society into a sacred arena. Ritual is the myth psycho-dramatically activated. The shadow side of the archetypes is engaged and the exalted side of the archetypes is called forth. Balance is restored. The shaman, who very often has to take this journey to heal himself, is the expert facilitating this process.

In this journey of restoration, humanity's first archetypes were introduced and reinforced, *i.e.*, the initiate, the warrior, the storyteller, the healer, the leader, the crone, the sage. These archetypes formed the structural guidelines for both the human psyche and societal occupation. While the realm of archetypes would become increasingly specialized with the hierarchies of Worlds Three and Four (*i.e.*, the priest, the priestess, the mystic, the King, the Queen, the magician, the ascetic, the Samaritan, the guru, the missionary, the entrepreneur, the civic leader), none of this older layer ever went away.

In tribal societies, there was generally not a strict dualism between good and evil. The intent, instead, was to move out of the shadow side of the archetype—the victim, the bully, the saboteur—into its more redemptive features. Such is the movement most of us moderns still make in our psychological work on ourselves.

These same imbalances, however, when not worked with in a conscious or benevolent enough way, could perpetuate all kinds of imbalances. This is the dark side, or what Jung called the *shadow*, and there are many historical instances when this shadow was embodied on a collective level (*i.e.*, Crusades, Inquisition, Jewish Holocaust, Cold War, Islamic/Judeo-Christian conflict, etc.)

World One didn't appear to suffer from this malady, perhaps simply because of the smaller scale of culture and conflict. The shadow marked the terrain of the light, the way out. Shamanic skills were about elucidating that journey. Most often, this was done by "willfully and skillfully" shifting consciousness. The shaman's clinical skills were, foremost, in the art of soul retrieval, a restoration of the parts of one's self that had never been given or allowed full expression.

The type of consciousness that pervades World One is what anthropology has called *magical*, although there have been limiting and ethnocentric perspectives attached to this term. Jung went beyond the pejorative interpretations of magical as "a make-believe fanciful world," and suggested the notion *synchronicity*, a kind of vibrational telepathy that indicates that human psyches are still deeply interconnected with each other and the natural world. Synchronicity suggests and confirms a *collective unconscious*, or again, what might be referred to by tribal cultures as the spirit world. Maintaining and manifesting this interconnection becomes the primary purpose of ritual and religion in the tribal world. In this work, this kind of consciousness is referred to as shamanic.

As indicated in surveys I conduct every semester with my Anthropology and Comparative Religion students, while shamanic cultures in their pristine state have pretty nearly been exterminated from the planet, this is still the religious form that most students readily identify with. This is not about non-natives becoming a bunch of "wannabes" (wanna be an Indian). It is about the cultural and psychological reservoir that we have all in common. Shamanic sensibility is laced into our physiology.

There is a kind of romanticism built into this. The freedoms of industrial society, of World Four, afford a choice to liberate oneself from the constraints of societal institutions, particularly religious ones. World One appears to be that liberation. However, World One, for all of its flexibility and attention to the needs of the individual, didn't have that freedom. People fit into the ritual cycles of their society, or they were often ostracized in some manner. What World One did offer was a kind of soaring archetypal journey, a process that still intrigues us today.

Linguists have demonstrated, in the European contact with the languages of tribal cultures over the course of the last 500 years, "that people from technologically simple societies are no less capable of expressing a wide variety of abstract ideas than are people living in high-technology societies" (Kottak, *Cultural Anthropology*, 2002). The modern has written much about the essentially unconscious state of humanity's first representatives. There were only a few, the shamans, who were truly conscious of the magic they were manifesting. It was the fruits of those talented few that moved humanity forward into the next world (Ken Wilber 1996).

To the contrary, *Apocalyptic Grace* suggests that there is a core consciousness, a core set of gifts and traits, inherent to the dawning of the species that have never left us. That gift is attunement. Through ongoing techniques of attunement a kind of expansion of consciousness was gained that set the foundation of the human psyche. The challenge, especially as the tower of the psyche grew more complex with each succeeding World, was getting back to the simple profound truths of this ground floor.

Medicine Wheel

In the recognition that we were now somehow apart from nature, but still of it, a ritually induced consciousness served to reconnect us to our web of relations—all that is, community, our intimate ones. It is that web which makes up the indigenous definition of self. The embodiment of this wisdom is what, in indigenous cultures worldwide, can generally be described as the Medicine Wheel. While the symbols and relationship of symbols of the Medicine Wheel would vary from tribe to tribe, the underlying principle remained constant. Balance.

The Medicine Wheel represents the seasons of nature, the solstices and the equinoxes, and their midpoints, that mark the passages of life. It is particularly those midpoints, what is known in the Celtic ritual cycle as *Samhain, Imbolc, Bealtaine,* and *Lunasa,* in which the veil between this world and the Spirit world is considered the thinnest.

What we see unfolding in this ritualized exploration of the links between human and "Mother" nature are the original templates of developmental psychology. A set of elaborate correspondences are established that serve as a linking of the passages of life (child, adolescent, adult, elder) and the seasons of nature (summer, autumn, winter, spring) with the development of the kinesthetic, emotional, mental, and intuitive realms. My teachers of this wheel have been, in chronological order, Kaylynn TwoTrees (1997), Joan Halifax (1988), Steven Foster and Meredith Little (1999). What I have learned from their applied wisdom, and my own personal integration of that wisdom, can be summarized as follows:

The Wheel starts in the South. What better time than summer to reflect on childhood. The world is discovered kinesthetically. A child doesn't want to read about it or be told about it. The child wants to feel the world in their body. Indeed, the child is often nothing but body and the world a magical extension of it. This corresponds with the behavioral/conditioning and biological aspects of modern psychology.

As the child matures, he or she moves into the West, the *Looks Within Place.* The sunlight is starting to fade; it is a time of going into the dark. The teenager is no longer a child, but not yet an adult. He is aware that he, too, will die one day. These are the psychodynamics of the psyche, the manner in which we grow ourselves up (or not).

This is the period that the Christian mystic St. John of the Cross referred to as the dark night of the soul. Feelings are overwhelming and force us to become more conscious of the depths of our emotional worlds. Without a powerful initiation into adult-hood, the darkness can become outright terrifying. The adolescent can get stuck. Sound familiar? This is the state that Jungians call *puer eternis,* the powerfully romantic but ungrounded drive to nev-er grow up.

The initiatory antidote is for the young adult to dive back into those depths, into "the ashes," to wrestle with one's own mortal-ity. From that stark engagement a deeper light, a deeper purpose emerges. In indigenous culture, it was a time to separate the ado-lescent from all other influences. It was a time to undertake a vision quest.

With no other distractions, the chatter going on in the head—the voices of Mom and Dad, peer group, societal and educational expectation—diminishes. The small quiet voice, the voice of the adolescent's terribly unique soul, emerges. The initiate begins to know and trust that voice. The bear held this space in the Medicine Wheel, for this was the time of the year when the bear prepared for hibernation, to go inside. Through this vigil, the adolescent begins to get comfortable with the dark side of their emotions.

In the North, the Medicine Wheel addressed the mature, care-giving, and problem-solving capacities of the adult. Symbolized by the Momma mountain lion, you don't want to get in between her and her cub. This is what psychology calls the cognitive, that abil-ity to process thought and solve problems. Having wrestled with the dark side, we are now able to be of service to our families and community.

The East, the elder, is the place of spiritual resting. The East provides an ongoing solace, a Light, and an assurance that there is a deep, compassionate reality encompassing all of our trials and tribulations. The East, also, is a type of knowledge, but unlike the cognitive nature of the North, a kind of an inner, intuitive knowing that takes a lifetime to manifest.

There's no training manual for Elderhood. There is, instead, a decades-long process of polishing and letting go. Represented by the Wolf, who is, at once, the *lone Wolf* (which is how we all must leave this world), and the *teacher*, the leader of the pack.

The Medicine Wheel served as humanity's first diagnostic manual. As delineated, the four poles I have just shared (the physical, the emotional, the mental, the spiritual) correspond with modern psychology's major orientations (the behavioral and biological, the psychodynamic, the cognitive, the archetypal and transpersonal). The Medicine Wheel operates within us at all times. That is why a child can sometimes come out with the wisdom of an adult, or an adult can sometimes act like a child.

When life gets out of balance, then its time to go to the other side of the wheel. For the child, this would be the adult, for the adolescent, the elder. The goal was to develop and balance all of these elements—the body, the heart, the mental, the spiritual as well as the child, the adolescent, the adult, the elder—within the context of one's immediate cultural surroundings and the planet's natural forces.

This process culminated in the elder's ability to organically synthesize all the different sensibilities and pieces of wisdom that had been digested over the course of a lifetime. In tribal culture, one didn't learn about the Medicine Wheel in the didactic way it is being presented here. It was introduced, rather, as one was ready for it, at the thresholds that World One cultures formally marked as rites of passage.

Whereas later systems of philosophy and religion would be channeled and written into elaborate and poetic texts, the Medicine Wheel was often embodied in *sacred sites*. The alignment of sacred sites was termed by metaphysical explorer Alfred Watkins as "ley lines" (Watkins, *The Old Straight Track*, 1925). It makes sense that sacred sites tend to be in the high (mountains) and low points (bodies of water, the desert) of a culture's immediate ecosystem. This is where "nature's energy" gathers.

Through a *cosmically* strategic building of dwellings and shrines, the principles of the Medicine Wheel were mapped out in the architectural relation of the community to its sacred sites. All is profoundly ordered. A central function of the cultures of World One was marking that awareness.

This occurrence was noted as old as 30,000 years ago in the Dordogne region of France. A bone inscribed with crescents and circles systematically marked the phases of the moon. Move forward to about 7,000 years ago and Medicine Wheel monuments were being constructed around the world. Britain's Stonehenge is the most notable example of this global awareness of a cosmic order governing our lives. This alignment, also known as *geomancy*, becomes the heart of World Two, but has its roots clearly sunk in World One.

The principles of the Medicine Wheel would deepen in World Two. As is the nature of World Two, rite of passage became an intense group bonding experience. Much of this would then get transferred into the rite of passage ceremonies provided by the emergence of the World Religions in World Three. World Four then undoes much of this. The modern—from the adolescent to the elder—is left thirsty for an explicit marking of the thresholds they are attempting to cross.

However, the same initiatory quest still gets played out through the operations and drive of the psyche. Particularly with the increasing alienation for the individual that hierarchal culture (Worlds Three and Four) introduces, what once was the subject area of anthropology now becomes psychology's domain. By hook or by crook, we will try to grow ourselves up. And if culture doesn't provide the ritual threshold to cross through, then we will often find a way to create one for ourselves (gang membership, subcultures, psychotherapy, assorted and combined spiritualities, popular culture).

I will suggest, however, that the same shamanic principles, however, are at work. We have to die to parts of ourselves in order to grow and move forward. The beauty of the Medicine Wheel and the rituals associated with it (vision quest, sweat lodge) is that it represents the anthropological and psychological common denominator that the entire species holds in common. Dive deep enough into the history of your cultural background, dive deep enough into your psyche, and you will land somewhere on the Medicine Wheel.

The Psychology of World One

World One culminates and is based on this notion of *Vision*. The actual name *Vision Quest* came from anthropologists noting this process among the Vikings of Scandinavia, and applying it to a similar ritual among the Plains Indians of North America. (Jesus going into the desert for forty days was a similar quest.) The general protocol of the ritual is to go out into the wilderness, in isolation without food, sometimes without water, with the intention of securing a vision. The soul, the unconscious, without the stimulation of culture and daily sustenance, will naturally provide one.

The Vision was uniquely individual, but, at the same time, taps into the symbols of the collective unconscious. In World One this was synonymous with the mythological landscape of the tribe. At its core, the psyche offers an ordered understanding, which, in turn, lends to a sense of life purpose.

The question is whether we can quiet ourselves—as the vision-quest ritual is designed to do—to allow this core to emerge. This is what the Christian tradition calls the "still, quiet voice." The implicit psychology is that there is an archetypal presence—one's traits, skills, and gifts—that each individual has the inherited choice to cultivate. World One culture enhances that cultivation.

Later wisdom traditions would call this ordering principle different things: the *Tao* of Taoism, the *Logos* of Christianity, the *dharma* of Buddhism. These are all culturally developed renditions of the coherence originally represented by the tools of World One:

the Medicine Wheel, the Vision Quest, the sweat lodge, and other purification regimes (herbology).

As we are now moving into the time of World Five, when so much is being reconsidered, it is no wonder that this ancient foundation, of both culture and psyche, should again receive attention. With the planet's advances of technology and ever growing populations, we will never return to a fully tribal way of life. However, the shamanic principles that sustained the first and longest chapter of the human story are still very much accessible.

🎝▷ Cultures of the Southwest
The Athabaskan Journey

According to anthropological theory, the Athabaskan peoples were the last migration of Asian peoples over the Siberian ice bridge to the North American continent. This occurred sometime around 500 hundred years CE. (The Hopi are adamant that other migrations came by boat, that the migrations went both ways, and there is archaeological evidence to support this.) The Navajo and Apache are the furthest migration south into the American Southwest of that Athabaskan population, although it is controversial when that actually happened (somewhere between 750 -1400 CE).

What is clear is that these people carry on a shamanic tradition akin to their Asian ancestry. I've met several Navajo who have traveled to Asia where they met people from the Mongolian region who had some of the same words in their spoken language. Although their exposure to and mixture with Pueblo culture fill in much of Navajo culture, their ceremonial core, to this day, is definitively World One in nature.

The essence of Athabaskan shamanic mastery is based on conscious dialogue between what the Navajo call the earth surface ones (us humans) and the holy ones, the latter an archetypal pantheon of forces. What is crucial is how well the individual and the group keeps up their end of the conservation (*i.e.*, prayers, offerings) with these spiritual entities and figures. It is ironic that these cultures have been called primitive when, indeed, their practical knowledge of the natural world was encyclopedic.

As these were oral cultures, these were masteries that had to be carried within memory and passed down from generation to generation. Using the traditional Navajo culture as an example, the number of terms for local herbs and plants was over a thousand (I'm lucky if I could name ten). The number of chants, embedded in a vast array of *chantway* systems that a medicine person had to know, was in the thousands. The *hatali* was one of the Navajo figures that anthropology would call a shaman. The hatali was the Ph.D. of Navajo culture.

Navajo sand painting exemplifies the transformative depths of Navajo ceremony. It is an embodied form of the Jungian technique of *active imagination*. As is the nature of World One shamanism, these ceremonies or "sings" are based around the needs of a particular individual. The sand painting is constructed after an initial four day purging of emotional and physical toxins (emetics, herbs, sweat lodges), a cleaning of the slate, so to speak, for the deeper healing to come.

This cleansing clues the elders in to then pictorially display what the dialogue between the earth surface and the holy ones for this particular person is about. Stated in modern psychological terms, this is the relationship between us humans and our enveloping archetypal forces. With the sand painting—which takes four to six hours to construct—the individual, the hero or heroine, then sits in the middle of the painting composed of their particular "holy ones."

The ongoing chants help drain the discordant energies back into the painting, which the holy ones can absorb. And finally, the painting is thrown back into earth as fertilizer. Fully utilizing the impact of symbol—the archetype in graphic form—on human consciousness and health, these ceremonies were truly the first psychotherapies. This was also Art Therapy 101. This was the emergence of the metaphoric mind.

The wisdom embodied in this initial thrust of culture goes something like this. There is a geomancy, an inherent ordering to the universe, that the Navajo called *hozho*. This was expressed in modern physics as "negative entropy." There is, however, as Murphy's Law acknowledged, the tendency for order to fall apart, what the Navajo called *hoxcho*, the physicist, *entropy*. This falling apart, what the modern theorist calls chaos theory, is as integral to the movement of the universe as the reality of and need for order. Indeed, there is a Navajo Ph.D. nuclear physicist, Fred Begay, whose parents were both traditional healers. He attributed his understanding of these laws of physics to his cultural knowledge of Navajo cosmology.

What links the falling apart and call for order in World One is ritual process, a conscious, concentrated engagement of the chaotic forces. This is what the Jungian would call engaging the shadow. Crucial for the journey is what the Navajo call *hoho ntseekee*s, the invitation "to think in beauty." This enlists the shadow, and the energy it steals, as an ally.

A similar motif is found among the ancient Greeks. There is a natural balance or justice, *dike*, to the universe, but that hubris and ate, arrogance and delusion, undo this. It is this downfall, what the Greeks called *nemesis*, that actually calls for a deeper balance. Our nemesis, as is the way of apocalypse, in bringing us to our knees, invites us into a more humble, true way of living. Dike, justice, hozho, and order are restored.

The Navajo archetypes, the holy ones, themselves have an interlacing nature of light and dark, good and perilous. There is a stern side to these deities, as with nature herself. A relation of reciprocity, of give and take, must be sustained between the earth surface and holy ones to keep this elusive equilibrium afloat.

This appeal and homage to the imaginal world lays down the foundation for humanity's core psychology. That the modern needs to spend more time getting in touch with and analyzing this imaginal world, *i.e.,* the psychoanalytic root of modern psychology, makes perfect sense. We've become a planet uprooted from a culturally cohesive divine imagination. The psyche, however, will still thrust forward, demanding an internal cohesion where culture can no longer supply it.

The shaman was simply better at doing what was inherent to the human condition, the ability to look deeper into different worlds, and to skillfully pass back and forth between them. To suggest that whatever was a skill back in untainted foraging cultures is now a relic, misses the point. Whatever humans once knew and learned can be remembered; whatever ritual humans practiced can be experienced again. Most importantly, the inhabitants of World One—like the Navajo—continued to grow alongside and amidst the changes introduced by Worlds Two, Three, and Four. We are all, by our very nature, culturally composite citizens.

I had a long conversation with R. Carlos Nakai, a Navajo musician who also claims Ute, Zuñi and Hispanic blood. Nakai was one of the first Native recording artists to receive international acclaim. He spoke of this culturally composite journey.

> Many people don't realize that Native cultures are a part of the earth changes that are happening, too, and that we can't be kept down in this 'traditional' niche that we've been put into. As Native Americans, we're always having to reevaluate and reestablish ourselves. It's not that we're actually throwing away or getting away from the old concepts but adding to them with our life experience at this moment in time. With the people outside the culture, we're not going to teach them how to become more like us, but, if anything, mirror back to them how to verbalize and be creative with the effect of removal from their own cultural contact with themselves. Some look to Native cultures for identity without realizing they have an identity that they were never allowed to express.

Hopefully, from this we can all build a greater cultural system out of what we all have been taken away from. (Interview with Nakai 1994)

Carlos Nakai
It's not that we're actually throwing away or getting away from the old concepts but adding to them with our life experience at this moment in time.

The indigenous person, if he so chooses, is as much a part of the modern world as the modern. The modern, if he so chooses to dive deeply into his own heritage and psyche, is, at the core, indigenous.

The indigenous cultures of the Southwest that still have their ceremonial cycles in tact (Pueblo, Navajo, Apache) have often done so by keeping a tight lid on what they should share, and what they should not. This has been their survival, their life-blood. On the other hand, another kind of indigenous sharing has been happening, a kind of pan-tribal sharing. We first see this in the Native American attempt to put down their tribal differences and unite under one Vision. If they didn't, their extinction could be imminent.

Personal Journey
Revitalization Movements:
The Ghost Dance and Peyote Religion

In my late teenage years I had a vision. I was combing through the anthropology section of the library at Temple University in Philadelphia where I was going for a degree in Comparative Religion. What caught my eye was a paper in *American Anthropologist* entitled "Revitalization Movements" (1956) by Anthony Wallace, the anthropologist who put this whole notion on the cultural map. While I found the whole work stunning, the following line particularly caught my attention: "Probably few men who have lived have not been involved in an instance of the revitalization process."

In a flash I understood that what happens in history is simultaneously happening inside us as well. Culture, our psychology, is being renewed. Two major revitalization movements of the last century and a half, the Ghost Dance Religion and the Peyote Religion, afforded an unprecedented opportunity for the budding profession of anthropologists to see new religions in the making. Rastafari was on their heals. Such is how culture regenerates itself.

Wavoka, known by his American name as John Wilson, went into a feverish trance amidst the eclipse of the Sun. The year was 1890. When he came out of it, this was the vision he shared:

> When the sun died, I went up to heaven and saw God and all the people who had died a long time ago. God told me to come back and tell my people they must be good and love one another, and not fight, or steal, or lie. He gave me this dance to give to my people. (Mooney, *The Ghost-Dance Religion and Wounded Knee*, 1991)

Within a six-month period, the vision had spread from the Paiute of the Sierras to the Cheyenne of the Rockies to the Sioux of the Plains. Altogether thirty to thirty-five tribes were infected. The Vision was sixty thousand strong. The message was unprecedented. Native American peoples needed to step beyond their ceremonial privacy and tribal differences and unite under One Vision. If they didn't, Native America was about to lose it all. Their numbers were dwindling due to disease and assimilation and American legislation was slamming down anything that smacked of barbaric ceremonialism. Through the Ghost Dance, a new religion was being created, a clever, visionary amalgamation of old and new ways.

What we see here is the central component of World One. The Vision Quest, a kind of collective dream state, allows for a pooling of memory and motivation. A way of life that was quickly being exterminated was revitalized in a way that integrated the contingencies of the World that was exterminating them. Jesus Christ, felt primarily as a crushing imperialistic force, was integral to that Vision.

> Do not tell the white people about this. Jesus is on the ground, he just like cloud. Do not refuse to work for white man or do not make any trouble.... I want you to make dance for six weeks. (Wavoka, in Mooney 1991)

> There are many Natives who regard the manner of his death as additional evidence of the White man's inhumanity, he not hesitated to attack the son of God. I never heard the

dance of the Indians called the 'Ghost Dance' until I returned to the East. In the Indian country, it is known as the Dance to Christ. (Mooney, Remarks recorded at Annual Meeting of American Folklore Society, November 1890)

A return of the ancestors was called for, but one, like this new Christian religion, that was entirely messianic in nature. This is the beauty and power of World One. It is entrepreneurial in a way that absorbs alien cultural influences. A new wholeness is created.

And yet, before the new religion ever left its infancy, the Ghost Dance was vanquished like the frontier, in an unfortunate hysteria of blood, fear, and mistrust. The Wounded Knee massacre of 1890 put an end to it. The Ghost Dancers thought they were impenetrable to the White man's bullets. They were not. James Mooney, an anthropologist actually on hand when the Ghost Dance occurred at the end of the last century, grasped the momentousness of what he was seeing:

> And when the race lies crushed and groaning beneath an alien yoke, how natural is the dream of a redeemer, an Arthur, who shall return from exile or awake from some long sleep to drive out the usurper and win back for his people what they have lost. The hope becomes a faith and the faith becomes the creed of priests and prophets, until the hero is a god and the dream a religion, looking to some great miracle for its culmination and accomplishment. The doctrine of the Hindu avatar, the Hebrew Messiah, the Christian millennium, and the leader of the Indian Ghost Dance, Wavoka, are essentially the same, and have their origin in a hope and longing common to all humanity. (Mooney 1991)

This visionary process is the kernel of World One's psychology that would serve, as well, all of the Worlds to come.

For all practical purposes, by 1900 the Ghost Dance could only be found in history books, government reports, and ethnographic reflections. Wavoka (John Wilson), the prophet and forger of the Ghost Dance vision, had gone into isolation with his wife. Wavoka, like a whole array of Native American shaman figures, consulted with a new Spirit sweeping up from Mexico. Another religion was about to be born.

The Peyote Religion

Somewhere in the Mexican desert began the sacramental use of what has been called "the diabolic root," "the key to the door of illusion," "the sacred plant and Spirit-path," "the Creator's road," and "the Way of Jesus." Its other names are multitude, but the most widely used and best known is peyote, from the Aztec word *petyotl* (La Barre 1989). The original use of peyote was among the pre-Columbian Indians of the highland Mexican plateau. The first Spanish explorers indicated peyote use by the now dispersed Aztec, and the Huichol, where today it is still very much a living religion.

The oldest reported use of peyote in the United States was among Native peoples whose land has since been named Texas. While this newer vision of what anthropology has come to call "the peyote cult" seemed to begin around 1870, its presence did not become fully conspicuous until nearly two decades later. Whereas the Ghost Dance preached of abandoning the present world in favor of regenerating a new one, the Peyote Religion advocated a turning inward, a Native parallel to the Christian's establishing the "kingdom within."

The Peyote Religion, has since been successfully defended by anthropologists in the U.S. Supreme Court, and has come to be known as the Native American Church. Peyote has become a legal sacrament. Its followers have formed the largest intertribal faith and practice aboard the planet. Like the Ghost Dance, it absorbed all that was in its path.

> After eating peyote, I grasped the meaning of the Bible, which before had been meaningless to me. We read in the Bible where Christ spoke of a Comforter who was to come.

Long ago this comforter came to the whites, but it never came to the Indians until it was sent by God in the form of this Holy medicine. The Christ talked to us in our respective tongues. (La Barre 1989)

Jesus Christ was alive and well on the Peyote road.

The Ghost Dance did not have much rooting in the Southwest. The Navajo had a particular fear of ghosts while the Pueblo's form of ceremony, as discussed in the next chapter, was focused on the group rather than individual vision. The notable exception was Taos Pueblo, whose geographical closeness to the Plains tribes also speaks of their genetic, linguistic, and cultural heritage. Unlike the other Pueblo peoples, a farming civilization that spread from the plains to the Grand Canyon, Taos Pueblo still adhered to the inner visionary core of their Plains Indian heritage. They practiced the Ghost Dance, and still practice the Peyote Religion. The Peyote Religion, meanwhile, spread like a wildfire among the Navajo in alliance with their visionary nature.

Whereas the Ghost Dance valiantly but naively tried to change the whole social landscape, the subsequent Peyote Religion was a bit more savvy. Building off of the intertribal network that the Ghost Dance created, the Peyote Religion understood that the main hope of revitalization, amidst an unrelenting World Four, was an internal spiritual revolution.

I couldn't help but notice a notable parallel to the Ghost Dance/Peyote Religion shift with the revolutionary hopes of the 1960s transforming into the self-help New Age revolution of the 1970s. The revolutionary idealism of the 1960s quickly went bust, so the only place to turn was to somehow manifest those changes in one's self. I wrote a senior honors thesis on the subject for my major in Comparative religion. It was called "Negotiations for a Heaven on Earth." It was supposed to be 40 pages. It turned out to be 162. It was my own Vision Quest. A few years later the whole vision came to the flesh.

Spirit Eagle

I first had extensive direct contact with a World One culture as supervisor of a community teen center in my late twenties. I helped to set up a cultural gathering between Telluride, Colorado youth and a group of Navajo teenagers from Shiprock, New Mexico. The supervisor of the Navajo group, Spirit Eagle, who was deeply involved with the "peyote spirit" had to suddenly leave due to his father's death. It was three months before I was again able to talk to him.

Navajo culture demands an extended vigil and vigilance around death. Traditionally, if the individual died in a hogan, then the structure was burnt down. What I learned was that Navajos believed that when spirit leaves the body, there is initially a volatile period in which those who have in any way been affiliated with that spirit must be cautious.

The Tibetans have made a science out of this. It is not that a person's spirit is "evil" or trying to seek revenge, but that there is an unknown, volatile quality about spirit, *i.e.*, another spirit may have attached itself on to it, and, thus, the living may require protection. With the proper guidance and protection, eventually the spirit travels to where and what form it is supposed to be next, and the vigilance relaxes.

I ended up taking care of those Navajo kids for the week, which was a marvelous way to do anthropology. I would ask them the nosy and naive questions I wouldn't dare pose to adults. My subsequent meeting with Spirit Eagle in his Shiprock, New Mexico, home was the beginning of my apprenticeship.

Both Spirit Eagle and his father are ceremonial leaders in the Native American Church. I say *are* because, as Spirit Eagle explained to me, when he looked at his father in their last ceremonial meeting together, he had transformed into an eagle and can still return in the form of that spirit. It was this archetype—the Eagle—that would come to me when I did ceremony in that same hogan.

While later participating in this type of ceremony in other locales, I would never feel that same type of immanent presence.

In sharing my work with Spirit Eagle, including this thesis I had written on the evolution of the Ghost Dance into the Peyote Religion, he couldn't help but chuckle. While he admired my passion, he frankly stated that I really didn't know anything about the Peyote Spirit. And then he mused, knowing that I was an anthropologist and a writer, "You and I could produce the next Carlos Castaneda series (the historical fiction account of a Yaqui shaman)." But suddenly Spirit Eagle was very serious. "Don't try to become like me. Look to your own ancestors. That's where your learning will come from."

And so I did. In the next few years, I learned to feel the presence of the spirit of my own deceased grandfather amidst the land and two cabins he built on it in the Finger Lakes Region of Western New York State. These were considered the sacred lands, indeed the birthplace of the Seneca Indians. An old Germanic tribal spirit appeared to me, a spirit softened by the Seneca land and Indian spirits, as was my grandfather. The spirit had the fierce and knowing presence of Wotan, the old Norse God that Christianity repressed as a kind of demonic pagan remnant.

This was the same archetype that Inquisitional Christianity pushed down in the Germanic psyche, and after World War I, came roaring back in the all too tragic form of fascism. This is what can happen to archetypes when they're banished and ignored. This is the same archetype Jung repeatedly noted in his analysis of post-World War II Nazis. Working through this clash of archetypal forces would become a lifelong journey for me and further described in the Worlds to come.

The American Vision Quest

In my apprenticeship with Spirit Eagle, I noticed an array of archetypal symbols adorning the walls of his father's hogan: Jesus Christ, Our Lady of Guadalupe, the Eagle, the Kennedy brothers, and the American flag. The religious ones made sense to me. In terms of Navajo survival, regardless of whatever threatening piece of history may be attached to them, the sacred archetypes possess their own unique and sacred gifts.

But the Kennedys and American flag did not go down so easily for me. After all, the Navajos were almost totally exterminated by the Long Walk in the 1860s, a campaign led by Kit Carson and the United States Army to round up all of the Navajo and Apache of the American Southwest and place them in a concentration camp outside of present day Fort Sumner, New Mexico.

The United States government tried to convert the Navajo and Apache into farmers, which was a miserable failure. These were hunting, gathering, and more recently, pastoral people, who were now succumbing to disease and despair. The Long Walk, in the Navajo and Apache psyche, remains a traumatic scar.

And yet, as Spirit Eagle explained, "My father understood that the American peoples were a visionary peoples, and the fact they chose the Eagle as their national symbol meant that beyond what has happened in history, the Vision still needed to be honored." Despite the imperialism, Spirit Eagle's father understood the freedoms proposed by World Four as a connection back to the visionary nature of World One.

The point has been made by Weston La Barre, the author of *The Peyote Cult* (1971) and *The Ghost Dance: The Origins of Religion* (1978), "that Western religion and much of its philosophy from Plato to Kant is the historical disintegration of the Ghost Dance of three great cultures, the Hebrew, the Greek and the Roman" (La Barre 1978). The tribal worlds of Europe and the Middle East were crumbling and being replaced by patriarchal hierarchies. The Abrahamic faiths, their thirst for knowledge and redemption, valiantly attempted to address and heal the oppressive consequences, but they, too, would be pulled into and propel the mission of Euro America's patriarchal regimes.

What Spirit Eagle's father was saying is that the American experiment must still be recognized for its visionary force. The Vision was not fulfilled and certainly took on some tragic twists, but as Spirit Eagle's father held forth, that cannot nullify the seeds and imperative of that Vision.

Onye Onyemaechi

Despite the wounding that has occurred between these two religious forms, the African tribal and the evangelical Christian, Onye has powerfully synthesized their spirit possession traditions.

73

The Anthropologist Gets Trance Possessed
Onye Onyemacci

Other profound entries into World One kept coming my way. I've been regularly attending a conference in Albuquerque, New Mexico on "Science and Consciousness." I am one of the "hired gun drummers" for Nigerian Onye Onyemacci, who regularly, through what he calls African-Christian mysticism, puts people into a trance.

This is what anthropology calls *spirit possession*. Despite the wounding that has occurred between these two religious forms, the African tribal and the evangelical Christian, Onye has power-fully synthesized their spirit possession traditions. The oldest healing techniques on the planet, the laying on of hands and talking in tongues, provided the connection. Onye had a way of slaying in the spirit even the most ardent disbeliever.

The workshops or evening celebrations would start innocently enough. When Onye first started coming here, some ten years ago, I was one of the few accompanying drummers. Now there is a global village of musicians, dancers, and supporters that corresponds with Onye's global vision. Once the rhythms kicked in and got a little heated, so would Onye's considerable charismatic light. While often invoking healing in the names of Mary and Jesus, it is clear Onye's outreach covers the evolutionary journey of the species. Helping guide Spirit into people's bodies and wounded souls, Onye has become the perfect and total embodiment of a modern day global shaman.

At this same conference, I attended a workshop conducted by an *Umbanda* Brazilian priestess. Anthropologically related to the African/Christian Caribbean syncretic blends of *Obeah, Santeria, Sango, Candomble,* and *Vodun,* Umbanda utilizes drums and chanting and a profound metaphysical understanding of the subtle realms. Encouraged to just "get into" and dance to the music, the last thing I remembered was the priestess coming up to me. Next thing I knew was there was an entourage of folks dressed in white encircling me. But then I realized they were actually stationary and it was I that was circling. I have no idea what the transition time was between the moment I was dancing and when I was whirling. It could have been seconds or minutes. I had blacked out. Spirit had possessed me.

I would later find out that the name of the ceremony was *gyra*, which means to whirl. That is what that spirit causes you to do when it enters into you. As the priestess explained, that spirit entered into me because there was already a resonance, an invitation, in my own soul for it to do so. As it turned out, the particular rhythm and chant was in homage to the forest, the geographic locale I have been attracted to and lived in most of my life.

Once confined to secret and esoteric circles, the spirit possession ceremonies of days past are surfacing in modern contexts. They must in order to heal the disparate abyss that all too often separates the modern psyche from its shamanic core. Even the outsider anthropologist gets swept in.

**Tina de Souza, Ph.D. Clinical Psychologist
and Umbanda Priestess**

*Once confined to secret and esoteric circles, the spirit possession
ceremonies of days past are surfacing in modern contexts.*

The Umbanda priestess, Tina de Souza, was also a Ph.D. clinical psychologist. She has her own practice back in Brazil, as well as students and satellite communities all over the world. Ms. de Souza had entered this religion when her brother was cured of a terminal diagnosis thirty some years ago, and they both have since dedicated their lives to it. This is the unique juncture we are entering. Indigenous knowledge is being approached and integrated in an entirely new way.

Trance, however, need not be so dramatic. Many of us enter it into it daily with our pets. At this same conference, noted biologist Rupert Sheldrake gave one of the keynote addresses in which he shared his latest studies and book based on the relationship of pet owners to their loyal canine companions (2000). Sheldrake demonstrated through time-synced cameras that dogs immediately sensed when their masters made the decision to return home (whether they were across town, the country, or an ocean) and went to the front door to wait for them. The communicative web that connected them and transcended time and space was love and devotion. This is the heart of World One.

🔲 Practical Applications

The World One cultures I have clinically worked with are the Navajo and Apache. There is a visionary archetypal quest that lies at the heart of World One, and so that is what is generally found in this type of client. There's much in the spiritual emphasis of World One that is at odds with the fragmentation of the industrial World Four. What was honored as a passionate journey to know thyself and to serve one's community from that gained knowledge must now be spun through the trauma all World One cultures have suffered. This can spill into all kinds of personality disorders. The shadow side of the passionate quest for Vision can show up as terrible repression, willful self-destruction, and/or bullying behaviors.

The therapeutic task with the World One client is to bridge the conflicting demands that the subsequent Worlds introduced. All challenge and conflict must be seen as part of the Vision Quest working itself out on a grander global scale. The client that comes to mind was a brilliant, young Navajo woman, torn between the Peyote Medicine ways of her father and the Pentecostal path of her mother. Each side of the family willfully put down the traditions of the other. This woman was split in half, torn between Worlds.

What I encouraged her to do was step outside the terrible conflicts this difference between Worlds has fostered. Pentecostal practice and belief, oddly enough, was one of America's first truly integrated Christian expressions between black and white followers. Beginning at the turn of 20th century, it reintroduced the shamanic trance possession experiences found in Jesus' first followers. There is an esoteric thread that laces this Pentecostal twist with the most ancient of World One religious experience. What I encouraged this client to do was to step outside the gossip mill, the shadow sides of both sides of her family, and experience the Peyote and Pentecostal paths as complimentary, not opposed.

World One is about humanity's core quest, to discover and follow your unique life purpose. World One is humanity's common denominator. Again, dive deeply enough into your own heritage and psyche and you will land there. The challenge for those having grown up within this culture is the understanding that the archetypes the modern world presents are considerably fragmented and diffused compared to the purity and intensity of original shamanic ritual. A magician energy is called for: the consciousness and ability to jump back and forth between worlds, to realize (real-eyes) that one's inner domain of meaning may not easily locate comparable reference points in the modern industrial world.

Inevitably, in World One, some of the plants that were gathered and the animals hunted were domesticated. Humanity was about to undergo its greatest revolution, the Neolithic. World Two had arrived. We decided to stay in one place and build houses. Soon they became villages and shortly thereafter, fortresses. In our minds, we have yet to dismantle them.

World One Summary

For over 90 percent of our time on the planet we have been hunters and gatherers. Men hunted. Women gathered. To a large extent, we still do. The gift the first layer of culture brings us is helping to put us in touch with our life purpose for community and ourselves.

Imagery, vibration, sound, all add up to a potential telepathic connection—what Jung called *synchronicity*—with all that is, or with whatever one wants to feel connected. World One utilizes this connection within the context of myth and ritual, so the central idea is to siphon tension off from everyday personal and societal pressures, and play out these tensions within a metaphorical and imaginal context.

This is, quintessentially, the journey of the hero/heroine.

Global Archetypal Unfolding

The Art of the Matter

The original archetypal awareness that accompanied the origins of the human species is discussed along with the globally universal cultural intention for humans to come into this awareness by systematically releasing stress out of the body.

"...da Original Funk..."

Cultures utilize ritual and myth to "siphon off" personal and social tension so as to facilitate personal and tribal healing.

Tracking the World: What a Tele-Pathetic Situation

The anthropological notion of *animism* links the indigenous notion of *spirit world* with what depth psychology works with as the *collective unconscious*.

Dying to One's Self

Jung's notion of the "transcendent function" is seen within the context of culture's push to sacrifice limited definitions of self to a greater communal and transcendent awareness. This is what anthropologist Victor Turner called *communitas* experiences.

Psychoneuroimmunology

The modern medical term of *psychoneuroimmunology* explains the profound shamanic understanding of the interaction of the body, the emotions, the thoughts and the spirit. Ritual and myth are then used to balance this body/heart/mind/spirit dynamic for both individuals and the community.

Medicine Wheel

The principles of the Medicine Wheel provide culture's original diagnostic tool and comprehensive model of the human condition.

The Psychology of World One

The World One drive to secure a Vision of how one is to live sets a psychological foundation that will serve all of the cultural Worlds to come.

🜚 Cultures of the Southwest
The Athabaskan Journey

Navajo ceremony is presented as an embodiment of the principles of World One.

❧ Personal Journey
Revitalization Movements: The Ghost Dance and Peyote Religion

An overview of two of Native America's most prominent revitalization movements.

Spirit Eagle
My personal journey with a Navajo Peyote Medicine Man.

The American Vision Quest
The Vision of American democracy corresponds to the ancient Vision Quest.

The Anthropologist Gets Trance Possessed
My experience with a Nigerian healer/drummer and a Brazilian Umbanda priestess.

▣ Practical Applications
Connecting with One's Life Purpose.

NEOLITHIC
REVOLUTION

WORLD TWO

Horticulture: There Comes
(and Goes) the Neighborhood

ADULT

Father Sky

ADOLESCENT
*Gods &
Goddesses*

ELDER
Ancestors

CHILD
Mother Earth

First Onset:

10,000 BCE — 3500 BCE

Predominant Infrastructure:

SMALL SCALE HORTICULTURE (HUMAN LABORED FARMING)

Predominant Social Structure:

CLAN, EXTENDED FAMILY, GOVERNING ASSOCIATIONS

Predominant Superstructure:

AGRARIAN BASED CEREMONIES, INITIATORY MYSTERY RELIGIONS

Predominant Medicinal Response:

COMMUNAL CATHARSIS, GEOMANCY

Predominant Mode of Thinking:

MYTHICAL

Human Potential Advance:

DEEP FEMININE / DEEP MASCULINE

Shadow Sides:

ANIMAL AND HUMAN SACRIFICE, SOCIAL CONFORMITY

American Southwest Culture:

PUEBLO

Personal Journey:

"DA FUNK," RASTAFARI, PUEBLO DREAMSCAPES

Global Archetypal Unfolding
The Neolithic Revolution

The next world comes upon us. Much that went for World One, the shamanic perception, goes here as well. Only now, everything deepens. The principles of the shaman are alive and well, but the shaman, slowly but surely, gets the rug pulled out from under him. In short, humanity begins to *domesticate nature,* and, in turn, itself. Villages, social structure, and ritual all become more pronounced. They become oriented around the agrarian year more than the individual need for healing.

The primary scientific endeavor of World One was an earth-based empiricism, a sophisticated observation of the healing properties of nature's ways and plants. As much of the power of the shaman's ritual was based around purification, these cultures became very adept at recognizing and cataloguing the intricacies of the natural world. Most notable was a widely employed herbology. This curiosity about nature's cycles would eventually lead to humanity's most momentous and treacherous shift: the Neolithic Revolution. The planet is still in recovery.

Cultural oppression has a long history. While original foraging cultures seem to have been as egalitarian as human society has ever been, there was evidence of a whole lot of "might makes right" going on as well. Most notable was the dominance of men over women, and of stronger men over weaker ones. But again, it was never a kill and conquer situation. It didn't have to be. If there was ever a significant challenge or clash, the nomadic peoples simply moved on.

With the advent of World Two, *territoriality* dramatically increased, as land was now fought over. Consequently, an unprecedented rise of warfare occurred, although still not in kill-and-conquer scenarios. A contagion of new diseases arose as well, as villagers were unaware of their own sanitation hazards. While some foraging peoples remained (although now nearly wiped out in their traditional form off the planet), they, too, were pulled into this un-precedented notion of "territoriality." The horticultural penchant for territory laid the groundwork for centuries of warfare to come.

In World Two, small clan "band" structures, based on a col-lection of nuclear families, shifted into extended families sharing common dwellings and tasks, and a larger overriding tribal orga-nization. Your daughter no longer just married a warrior. She also married a farmhand. And the more farmhands, the merrier.

The profession of shaman gives way to a priestly class. How-ever, many of the same shamanic principles stayed intact. Indeed, even with the advent of the world religions—the fruits of World Three—these principles never quite go away. They were simply reconfigured in new contexts. Indeed, if you look at the Christian calendar, many of its special times and events are formerly pagan "mythic" occasions (the word *pagan* actually just meaning "villag-er") that were simply given Christian window dressing. Christmas is Winter Solstice, the Easter Bunny symbolic of what it is that rab-bits like to do with the fertile arrival of the Spring planting season.

Consciousness intensifies in World Two. It has to. There was more complexity and regularity. The planting and cultivating of seed demands such. A deeper understanding and administering of order, both Cosmic and societal, was at hand.

The ancestral link deepens. It makes sense, as peoples, once nomadic, become sedentary, burying and living with their dead in the same proximity for generations. The relationship, as one would expect, to the earth also deepens and hence these horticultural so-cieties all over the world get the reputation of being matriarchal cultures.

But, curiously, the relationship to the sky gods, to the mascu-line, deepens as well. *Megaliths* go up and *kivas* go down. Yin/Yang, Shiva/Shakti, Mother Earth/Father Sky, become all encompassing ways of life. The psyche, the *self*, becomes more domesticated, but not quite the ego/mental setup that World Three would introduce and World Four emphatically reinforce. There begins a paradoxical surfacing of more communal activity and yet a more conscious and contained sense of self. This is what streams of religions and a branch of modern psychology have come to call the **soul**.

Earth Changes

These changes started long ago. The climate warms. Glaciers, the end of a long Paleolithic age, recede. Around 8,000 BCE, the landscape shifts accordingly. Bigger game animals begin to disappear. Whereas the more northern cultures would go through deprivation, others—those now based around river valleys in China, Southeast Asia, India, the Middle East, and Central and South America—would miraculously flourish. In fairly rapid succession, sheep, dogs, goats, pigs, turkeys, and eventually cattle, would come under humanity's thumb. The cultivation of roots, grains, and legumes equally ensued.

Whereas calendrical systems were in place, due to the planning nature of agricultural activity, a whole new kind of attention and precision had to be brought to this existing knowledge. Time, as we know it today, was born. Past, present, future, became more distinctly marked, although still played out within the eternal cycles of the sacred and the profane. If this calendar of events was not adequately paid attention to and acted upon, there would be dire consequences, *i.e.*, the loss of crops, down the road. A priestly class, priding itself on a combination of astronomical and agrarian insights, was in the making.

Hunting continued, of course, but more and more time became delegated to protect the fields either from marauding animals or humans. The archetype of the peaceful farmer has long lulled humanity into the prospects of a less bloody vegetarian-governed world, but a contrary truth seems to disturb this image. Whereas the hunter in foraging culture brought forth the original warrior archetype, territory in horticultural society must now be acquired and defended. Hence, there came an unprecedented rise in the rate of warfare and the creation of military organizations. The farmers' villages began to serve also as fortresses.

The first diseases of civilization, the increased lack of sanitation and contagion of staying in one place, also enter into the picture. With war and disease breaking out in epidemic proportions, this darkness, subsequently, will never leave humanity's side. World Two naturally develops ritual practices to mirror and offset this devouring side. These new prospects and terrors of culture invited an intensified, imaginative response. Such were the seeds of the shift from magical to *mythic* consciousness.

The symbols began to turn up everywhere. Starting in Central Asia, they spread westward to Europe and Africa, and eastward to southern Asia and the New World. Indeed, there is anthropological evidence that all of humanity's DNA, after making the march out of Africa, can be traced to Central Asia. This was humanity's crossroads.

Icons such as the ancient swastika, the double ax, and the labyrinth that served as the foundation of East Indian yogic mastery turn up in the same time period, halfway around the world in Greece. As the discipline of archeology is still trying to fill in the gaps, a Neolithic consciousness was encircling the planet. Though differing in texture and cultural motifs, the thread was unmistakable.

The divine masculine is represented by the bull, the snake, the ram, the erect phallus, and most dramatically megalithic monuments reaching to the sky. Becoming more attuned to and actually recreating nature's cycles of rebirth, the agricultural awareness naturally invited a greater understanding of death. But in World Two, the Goddess predominates, represented foremost by the mother earth that agriculturally sustains us.

At about 5000 BCE megalithic structures, mammoth stone formations pointing to the sky, popped up around the world, a spread from Britain and the Mediterranean to Algeria and Palestine, to Ceylon, Tibet and Korea. England's Stonehenge is the most renowned. These were ceremonial markers navigating the life of the soul beyond its worldly existence. Since entire cultures were now burying and living with their dead in sedentary agricultural communities, it made perfect sense to build monuments where the departed had a place to hover and rest. These were the planet's first tombstones.

World Two viscerally participates in the same cyclical destiny of the seeds they planted: birth, life, death, and rebirth. These huge blocks of granite served as the invitation and site for ritualized communion with the ancestors. Ecstatic rites, built in the East around the masculine/feminine nucleus pairing of figures like Shiva/Shakti or, in the West, the Eleusian and Dionysian mystery cults, ensured the vitality of that communion.

In the East, this would form the foundation of Hinduism, although the religion would not formally get its name until the 19th century arrival of the British. A deeper refuge, a communal ecstasy, was now sought. In the West, much of the symbols and rituals of the Greek mystery religions would feed into the Abrahamic faiths, particularly New Testament Christianity. As will be explored further in the next chapter, these same faiths would then go to great lengths to disavow their own essentially shamanic foundations.

Similar shamanic themes and ecstatic activities would play out in Northern Europe among the Druids, and be incorporated within a Celtic-colored Christianity. The Druids were a Celtic priestly caste comparable to the Hindu Brahmins. They held grand initiations on the two equinoxes and solstices and, lo and behold, a festival held on December 25 announced the birthday of the sun god Sol.

Whereas East Indian culture would refine the understanding of this ecstatic knowledge through the Vedic literature, earlier indigenous horticultural societies seem to be where these revelations began. What all of these expressions conveyed—Druids, Greek Mystery Religions, early Hindu ceremonialism—is, again, a dying to something greater than oneself; a dying and rebirth intrinsically linked to the *focused frenzy* of group ritual.

Mything It Out

We all have a story to tell. This is, quintessentially, human nature. The agrarian cycle, the regulated ability to plant and create sustenance on the material plane, equally created a regulated cycle of myth and ritual. Ceremonies, based in foraging cultures on attending to individual needs, now served to demarcate time and assure that the community is in alignment with nature's cyclical changes. In this aligning with time and timely parts of the year—the equinoxes and solstices, the planting and the harvesting—a whole new leap in consciousness emerges. In our ability to coerce and manipulate nature, we become more proud, more aware, of ourselves as distinctly human.

In so doing, our supreme archetypal reflections, once more beholden to the animal world, become anthropomorphized into an increasing dazzling array of human-like deities. Pantheons of Gods and Goddesses (Greek, Egyptian, Iranian, Aztec, Celtic, African, Maya, early Hindu, etc.) erupt. Just as the sedentary lifestyles of World Two create a geographically more fixed cycle of shrine and ceremonies, the myths, once a kind of roving medicine bag of stories, become more pronounced. Their plotlines thicken. In so doing they also threaten to turn into dogma.

All mythologies seem to fold into the structure of the original myth: a fall from paradise and the quest (for consciousness) to reverse that fall. Nothing is merely what it is. It points to a greater meaning beyond itself and the stories, the myths, remind us of what is and might be. Point blank, failure is confessed in our myths, and, therein precisely lies their function. Myths harmonize with the world not as it appears, but as how the collective imagination wants the world to create itself.

Myths also lend human intention and deed a natural cause and a natural conclusion. Even amidst the banalities of the modern world, we are always cranking out mythological tales inside ourselves to explain, clarify and glorify our existence. We can't seem to stop doing this. It's a kind of inborn response to the challenges and joys of the day.

Myths are by nature transformative, pulling us out of the incongruities of the moment into a world that, for better or worse, makes sense. Henceforth, whatever is meaningful about human activity, if not part of a consciously expressed myth, conforms to a deeper mythological structure. In portraying humanity's intrinsic incompleteness this structure anticipates and projects this completion. Foremost myths tackle the most extreme contradictions—our failures despite the quest for success, our sicknesses despite the quest for health, our wars despite the quest for peace—and make them palatable.

Myths resolve the tension of the opposites. In so doing, they set the foundation for how humanity—despite all its shortcomings—explains itself.

> Ultimately it is the wish to recover this lost unity that has caused man to think of the opposites as complementary aspects of a single reality. It recurs under various aspects and all levels of cultural life— in mystical philosophy and theology, in the mythologies and folklore of the world, in the modern's dreams and fantasies and in artistic creation. (Eliade, *A History of Religious Ideas*, 1978)

In Worlds One and Two mythology amounted to a collective dream state, what the Aborigines refer to as *dreamtime*. A kind of "natural law" bound the consciousness of the people, and it was the elders and shamans that would help the tribe tap into that awareness.

Whereas the forager's World was more nature oriented, the horticulturist's World becomes more anthropomorphically soul centered. The Gods and Goddesses all look rather human like. Whereas the forager tended to create and improvise upon myths as needed, with horticultural societies, the myths, as does the social structure, becomes more fixed. People conform more to the myths than the myths to the people.

Mother Earth

The cultural tide had shifted. An unprecedented ritual power, the growth of villages, of governing associations, and a binding social conformity, was the result. Increasingly aiding that process, along with an expanding anthropomorphized mythical consciousness, was an equally expanding technology: the spade, the plow, the mining of the earth.

> All over the world miners practice rites involving a state of purity, fasting, meditation, prayers, and cult acts. He (the miner) has the feeling that he risks entering a domain that does not rightfully belong to man: the underground world with its mysteries of the slow mineralogical gestation that takes place in the womb of Mother Earth. All the mythologies of the mines and mountains, the countless fairies, genii, elves, phantoms, and spirits, are the multiple epiphanies of the sacred presence that the individual confronts when he penetrates into the geological levels of Life. (Eliade 1978)

The rhythms of ceremony and work, of technology and sustenance, were bound within the parameters of the sacred.

A 19th century Native American responded to the World Four capitalist agenda of the conquering Euro-American peoples in mythological terms:

> You ask me to plough the ground? Shall I take a knife and tear my mother's bosom? Then when I die she will not take me to her bosom to rest. You ask me to dig for stone? Shall I dig under her skin for her bones? Then when I die I cannot enter her body to be born again. You ask me to cut grass and make hay and sell it, and be rich like White men. But how dare I cut off my mother's hair? (Eliade 1978)

This passage indicates the *natural law* still prevalent in the horticultural world.

The shift between World One and World Two comes down to this. World One is about Vision, the life purpose that individuals seek, particularly in relation to all of the other relations that shape us: family, community, all that is. In the forager's dance, you want to kick your heels up—fancy dancing—a reflection of the unique light that shines within each of us. With this emphasis on individuality, World One sets a mighty precedent for the entrepreneurial, capitalist World Four.

In contrast, World Two is how well we work together on the land and in ceremony. There's a different kind of power at work, the kind of synchronicity and beauty modeled by a flock of birds in flight. When one bird changes courses, they all change course. Seamlessly. In the horticultural dance, you don't want to stand out, and will be reprimanded for it. Its how well you tap into and move with the flow of the group.

World Two sets precedent for modern democracy as well as the socialist critique of a self-serving capitalism. Thomas Jefferson, a prominent founder of modern democracy, was well aware of the Confederation of the Iroquois Nation. He couldn't help but notice democratic ideals at work. Six Native American nations, once in tension and at war with each other, worked together effectively and harmoniously.

In this anthropological light, the modern political equation becomes fairly simple. The individualism/capitalism (of Westernized nations) of World Four finds its roots in the individualism of World One. The reverence for and power of the collective, World Three (Islamic and Communist Nations), finds its roots in the group solidarity of World Two.

These are flip sides of the coin of human nature. Much of the individual needs of World One now get taken care of by the emphasis on the personal self in World Four. The journey is still about finding and fulfilling purpose. Much of the needs of World Two are now being met through popular culture, the forms of cathartic arts, entertainment, and religious possibilities that bring us together into group consciousness. World One and World Two form the right and left legs, the *foundation*, of the human experience.

The Origins of Formal Religion

In World Two, the Goddess arrives full-tilt boogie. Since women were now playing a crucial role in the domestication of nature, they became the proprietors of the fields and the homes. The fertility of the earth became linked up with the fertility of the women. Together they formed the divine feminine mystery called life and thus received special attention and worship.

The man, out of societal necessity, paid humble homage to the feminine—or there could be much greater losses to be had. The destructive side of the feminine, of Mother Nature, had to be appeased. There was, however, as we see manifest in some manner in all of the Worlds, a shadow element that would come into play as well.

> Worshipped from Egypt to India, from Greece and Asia Minor to darkest African, the Great Mother was always regarded as a goddess of the chase and of war; her rites were bloody, her festivals orgiastic. All these features were essentially interconnected. (Newmann, *The Origins and History of Consciousness*, 1954)

Human sacrifice was a part of this mix. While this time period stands out as the more matriarchal of our history, the goddess figures also had a devouring side. All of this bloodshed spoke of a desperate appeasement of the Great Mother, a destruct and/or self-destruct mode that still speaks to the kind of transcendence that encourages people to die for a cause.

For many World Two cultures, the tribal center no longer held. Beginning as the shift into unprecedented group solidarity, the party got out of hand. The priests started taking power that formally was the domain of the Gods. The priests, once stepping in and out of their roles as ceremony dictated, start becoming an entrenched social class. They rule over the warriors and peasants below them. People began taking control over other people's lives.

Formal religion doesn't start to show up until the spiritual integrity of the tribe begins to fall apart. What was supposed to be the fruits of World Two began to decay. The egalitarian foundation of culture was betrayed. Redistributive chiefdoms turn into hording nobilities. The first monarchies were aboard the planet. In short, the tribal world goes amuck. *Sin* is an archery term defined in Jesus of Nazareth's native tongue of Aramaic as "missing the mark."

This sense that something is amiss becomes an entrenched element of the human condition. The tribal world turns it's expanding demographic into conquering warfare. This is the historical stage the Old Testament describes, tribe pitted against tribe, humanity against itself. Hierarchy would bring more order, but less justice, to this scene. A new tension of the opposites emerges, a more individualized set of heroic journeys pitted against an unjust world.

The world becomes a much more daunting and isolating place, but now filled with all kinds of adventures to get us out of our predicaments. The rise of social injustice, coupled with the loss of tribal solidarity, causes the human psyche a whole new kind of anguish. Our emotional worlds become increasingly *shame based*. We feel naked, rather than belonging, in the Garden of Eden.

The horticultural myths begin to account for these "transgressions" that were happening. The universal uniting of the Earth Mother and the Sky Father was threatened by a whole new kind of mythic story that spoke of their splitting apart; a separation that also carries the unprecedented human possibilities of loneliness and rejection. The mythic plotline responds accordingly, a universal story about a flood, a fallen people suddenly submerged under water. It would take heroic effort—indeed, the emergence of the hero/heroine, to bring resolution to a whole new malaise that humanity was now feeling.

In the domain of the psyche, how this tension plays itself out is an unprecedented quest for liberation. And yet, it is this lunge for Oneness that can also trap culture. Human sacrifice is the prime example. It is those individuals who embody the *puer eternis*, eternal youth, who most often get sacrificed for a greater seductive force. An evolutionary maturation, cultural and personal, however, is also in the wings.

What culture introduces with one hand, it tries to repair with the other. **The cultural and archetypal potential that World Two introduces reaches fruition in the world religions of World Three: the sacrifice of the *puer eternis*, no longer on a bloody physical plane, but a spiritually redemptive one.** We see this prescribed in Hinduism's *Upanishads* as "the interiorization of sacrifice." What was to be sacrificed was no longer an outer human or animal, but the inner "base" parts of one's self to one's more exalted self, or what modern twelve-step groups call "a higher power."

The emergence of the ego as the center of the self was just as swiftly spiritually dethroned. Kali, with her garland of human heads, is the perfect symbol of this. While the imagery may seem severe, so is Kali's message: The human ego is too tainted to run the show.

This transition out of blood-infested sacrifices can be found in the emergence of maturated goddess figures (Kali and Durga in the East, the Greek Demeter, Melaina, Cybele, and Diana, or the later Christian Black Madonnas) that could hold this tension—sheer life, sheer destruction—of the opposites. The mythical story of Kali choosing not to fully to destroy the world because her lover, Shiva, is brave enough to show up to beg her not to, captures this tension. (Shiva, however, still ends up under Kali's foot). Not acting out upon this tension allows "the transcendent function" to again shine forth. The elimination of sacrifice is what will uniformly link the emergence of the world religions in World Three.

The Psychology of World Two

The psychology of World One was about establishing an individualized archetypal presence amidst the regressive pressures of the psyche. A greater mother and father were cosmically established as a backdrop and anchor for the psyche to fulfill a greater wholeness. World Two continues much of this, but the emphasis is now on a group versus individual consciousness, with more attention paid to a greater array of anthropomorphized (human-like) deities. The psyche, as does our personalities and societies, becomes more complex.

Myth, a sense of the way things are supposed to be, establishes a greater binding authority. The results are mixed. On the one hand, cultures lean towards a greater organizational competency. The village structure is born. On the other, there is a kind of social conformity that will begin to chain in the soaring archetypal journeys characteristic of World One. Consequently, there is a persistent personal feeling of transgression, what the Old Testament refers to as sin, and these new myths record as a kind of fall from paradise. The increasing psychology is the felt sense that something is wrong with us, a malaise that will continue with us to the modern world.

World Two's unconscious shadow response was to sacrifice members of its own societies, particularly the adolescent shining stars, as a way of appeasing what felt like the unhappy Mother of the Universe. The shadow, however, starts to integrate itself in a more conscious fashion, the sacrifices shifting instead to becoming more conscious of, and diminishing the unworthy portions of, one's self. Whereas the group could be a coercive factor, in this new integration it can also provide a supportive, cathartic push into a greater freedom.

Such is the psychological tension us moderns continue to face in relation to the group pressures of our societies. Be it family, peer or institutional, there is the constant sense that something always has tabs on us. We can't help but feel like we've just done, or are about to do, something wrong.

Tribalism, the shadow side of any group, is as much with us today as in its indigenous roots. The redemptive side of the tribe is the modern's ability to pick which groups might facilitate their own healing, and to enter or leave them as one chooses. As much as us humans might like to think otherwise, the findings of psychology indicate that we simply cannot do this journey alone. The group quickly reminds us we are not the only one going through what we are going through, and helps shrink our self-importance and anguish about that. As World Two seemed to irreversibly imprint into our physiology, we are culturally wired to be in relationship. Without good relations, our wholeness will continue to elude us.

Now let us see how this dynamic plays itself out in a classic World Two culture, the Puebloan.

Cultures of the Southwest – The Puebloan
The Anasazi Didn't Go Anywhere

The Puebloan peoples are considered one of the oldest in the New World. Arriving in the American Southwest at least 12,000 years ago, these were big game hunters of varying languages and customs. What brought them together under the cultural umbrella of Puebloan was a shift prompted by the recession of the last ice flow. The weather turned dramatically drier, with many of the bigger animals going extinct.

Around 2,000 years ago, a farming culture flourished that stretched from modern day Las Vegas, New Mexico, to Las Vegas, Nevada, and from Durango, Colorado, to Durango, Mexico. This was the Rome of the Southwest. (While referred to in the older literature as the *Anasazi*, as this is a Navajo term that pejoratively refers to the "ancestors of our enemies." It has since been dropped in favor of Puebloan.)

The peak of Puebloan culture occurred with "the Chaco Phenomenon," a geographic and sacred center of pilgrimage and homage that was built smack dab in the middle of outlier communities and the entire Pueblo cultural spread. From Hopi in the West to the Rio Grande Pueblos in the East, from Zuñi and Acoma to the South, to Aztec and Mesa Verde to the North, the Pueblo cultural wheel inhabited the entire American Southwest. Chaco Canyon was the hub of that wheel.

Built roughly between 800 and 1200 CE, one structure, Pueblo Bonito, contained the most numbers of rooms (800-plus) anywhere, until a 19th century Chicago apartment building. These ancient masonry sites were built entirely without instruments, perfectly aligned to solar and lunar seasonal movements. The rigor of scientific method, a precise regulated observation of nature's ways, was the order of the day.

Ley lines were drawn onto the earth. Wider than the roads connecting the 75-plus Chacoan communities as transport for goods and information, these ley lines seemingly ended nowhere. They were actually, however, tracing the geographic energy flows of the American Southwest, a circular outreach that made Chaco Canyon the natural geographic center. Ley lines are to the surface of the earth what acupuncture meridians are to the body. Chaco was the *hara*, the energetic power center, of the Puebloan world.

Puebloan culture has its roots in Mesoamerican culture, particularly the Maya. It was there that a natural grass, *teosinte*, was domesticated as corn and migrated to tribal communities on all ends of the American continents. Like their Mesoamerican cousins to the south, the Maya, the center did not hold. People left en masse from what may have been a harsh hierarchal turn. The have-nots got tired of the haves. As rainmaking was dependent on harmoniously working communities, prolonged drought most likely contributed to this mayhem. Chaos reigned.

Again, like the Maya, the Pueblo opted for their earlier small-scale horticultural way of life. It was that rare instance where evolution chose to go backwards, a return from complexity to simplicity. The Anasazi, however, did not disappear, as some earlier histories (previous mythologies) have suggested. These people are alive and well as the acknowledged descendants of the Chacoan culture and phenomenon. They are the current day Puebloan peoples.

What united the Puebloan cultures was not a common origin, as to this day there are at least four completely distinct languages (Tanoan, Keres, Zuñi , Hopi) emanating from opposite directions of the American continents. Instead, the uniting factor was the mutual turn to horticulture and a ceremonial harnessing of weather.

What was created was a fairly uniform ritual form based around the *kiva*, the ground-centered ceremonial chamber that serves as an umbilical cord to Mother Earth. Pueblo culture is not a nation, and never was. These are autonomous communities linked by the imperatives and practices of World Two.

Weather Making and Ancestral Connection

The crowning of this culture was the ability to create *weather*, a necessary ingredient to sustain farming culture in the dry Southwest. *Kachinas* are represented by the masks dancers wore during ceremony, or the dolls given to the children as a way of teaching the culture. The underlying meaning, however, of kachina was the *form* by which spirit manifests. As a Yaqui Indian, Fidel Moreno, shared with me, a meeting held with meteorologists and Native American elders in Albuquerque, New Mexico, on why rain dances might even work came to the following conclusions:

> When we do ceremony, we augment and enhance, individually and as a collective, our electromagnetic field. This field is what makes the Universe of World Two tick and hold together. The best thing one can become in the Pueblo world after passing away is a cloud. Ancestral spirit, diffused back into nature, coalesces through the power of the ceremony. Clouds form. It rains.

The kachina, etymologically meaning "respect of spirit," is of this spirit world that Pueblo horticultural societies pivot upon. And while modern science is still trying to catch on to why rain dances might actually work, from the indigenous perspective it is a vibrational mimicry aligned with the homeopathic principle of like attracts like.

The rattling, the movement, and the singing mimic and call forth rain. Through ceremony, the communities, in terms of sheer mechanical physics, are becoming magnets. Ancestral spirits, in the form of clouds, are electromagnetically responding to the community's call.

Okay, believe what you will! But here is my own experience of this phenomenon. I used to live near Glorieta, a half-hour to the east of Santa Fe, New Mexico. There was a pithouse right in my backyard that no archeologist had ever seen, as there were sites and artifacts strewn over the entire Glorieta plateau. The pithouse was a structure dug into the earth, a home, but also the forerunner of the kiva. There is a metropolitan strip of these New Mexican Puebloan sites on both sides of the Rio Grande that stretch from Socorro to Taos.

I used to walk my dog through the adjacent fenced-off lands. When I went through one section, I felt like I was being watched, that there was, for lack of a more scientific description, a *twinkling energy* surrounding me. One day a sign was placed on the fence that said "Jemez Tribal Lands." The few remaining people of the Pecos Pueblo (ten miles down the plateau) abandoned their home in 1838 to be with their Jemez Towa speaking relatives eighty miles across the valley. Recently the Pueblo has been fighting to get lands back on this plateau because this is, they claim, where their ancestors are.

This again is not simply a poetic metaphor, although the Natives, with all of the ridicule and persecution they have received around this issue, were fine to let the White people believe it as such. Sure enough, I came home one evening and I heard drumming. The nosy anthropologist that I am, I sneaked over to the tribal lands and they were drumming in the very grove where I had confirmed our respective "twinkling energy" experience.

Members of the Jemez Pueblo had come back to that very grove to reconnect and pay homage to the ancestral spirits they knew were still hanging out there. They had known precisely where their ancestors were still hovering. This sensitive perception is a glue that holds these cultures together.

It was precisely because of these practices and beliefs that the Inquisitional entry of the Spanish and the science-bound mind of the Anglo denigrated these cultures. The modern world has not yet developed the technology to be able to understand or record this ancient science, this ancient knowing. Beneath the modernization and trauma, this sensitive kind of seeing and sensing still lies at the core of Pueblo culture.

The stories kept rolling in. A brand new mid-1990s Native American preparatory school had been built farther down this same plateau. They decided during the first week to take their students to the ancient Pecos Pueblo, a site partially restored courtesy of former landowner and actress Greer Garson convincing her friend, President Ronald Reagan, to turn it into a National Monument. The kids went down into a restored kiva, as though this were some kind of novel educational activity. In fact, many of them had grown up, back at their own Pueblo communities, within the esoteric activity of kivas.

They returned to the boarding school that night reporting of visions and voices. The Native American parents got wind of the event, were terribly irate, and the school was closed in a week. Eventually the school reopened, having publicly repented for their cultural mistake. What was an educational artifact in one culture was a still a living entity in another.

A few years later, many of the relics and artifacts that archaeologists had removed from the site were now returned, via the legal imperatives established by the 1990 Repatriation Act. The Jemez people, including children and elders, walked the eighty miles to meet that return and then, in closed ceremony, re-interred the ancestors. For Pueblo communities, the connection with ancestral realms remains vibrationally alive, and is crucial for their cultural survival.

To this day, the spread of Pueblo culture represents the spectrum of World Two. The communities to the West (Hopi, Zuñi) still maintain the more ancient, egalitarian matriarchal structure. What might be interpreted as anarchic is actually an interwoven governmental set of clans that provide natural checks and balances on each other. The Keres, located southwest of Santa Fe, become more centralized, but still carry on many of the ancient medicine societies. Among the Tanoan communities, hugging both sides of the Rio Grande, there's a definitive turn to patriarchal communities, a forerunner of World Three to come.

Edutainment

The irony of Pueblo culture is that many of the more successful individuals in the modern world, or what might be incorrectly interpreted as "assimilated," are those who have kept their traditional culture the strongest as well. While certainly still dealing with their share of cultural trauma and dysfunction, as a whole the Pueblo have become a model for the world in their ability to cross back and forth between Worlds.

Robert Mirabal, a Taos Pueblo artisan and world-renowned musical entertainer, perches himself on this cutting edge. Having seen him grow up on stage, Robert evolved from a feisty and, at times, a seriously depressed adolescent heavy metal fan to a marketed New Age flute player/maker to the accomplished world musician he now is. He has had to face both praise and condemnation from his tribe in his efforts to step out of his community's horticultural box into a greater, synthesized reality.

Some have felt Robert, as an entertainer, has shared tribal ways that should be reserved only for their tribe. This tension has characterized most modern Native communities, particulary with the increasing advent of non-Native outsiders curious about tribal ways. Robert shared these thoughts with me:

I grew up inside the Pueblo walls. The way that we lived and the way that we were—those days are gone. What I've done is create controversy. If it is controversial, then on some level we are growing. The destruction, the earth changes that are happening now, are a new way of realizing that we are not

Robert Mirabal

The destruction, the earth changes that are happening now, are a new way of realizing that we are not in charge… a way of inviting people to come together in a new way.

in charge. It's a way of inviting people to come together in a new way, to create a realization that there is another way of thinking, another way of expression, where we deliver hope back into the world. The only way we are going to evolve is by learning what the pain and suffering are about.

One thing that has given me a lot of power is that I don't mind being a fool. There are interesting beliefs worldwide in the archetypal hero of the fool, a figure who shows up in our culture as Kokopelli (the mythical flute player who shows up in petroglyphs and spreads his seed throughout the Americas). And so, if I am a fool in becoming a rock star and also being of my culture, so be it. The rock concert has become our modern day church. It is just like our ceremony in that we are creating the sweat and the stomp and trying to represent everything for the higher good. Spirit goes into me and out of me and into you. In the very end, we all have the same roots to return to. If we can all honor one another no matter where we come from, then there is a possibility that maybe we can help one another, a human global way of thinking.

As evidenced in the last century's outpouring of popular musical culture, the communal celebratory aspects of the horticultural world have come full circle.

Nearly all World Two cultures would either be colonized by or grow into the regimes of World Three. This shows up for the Pueblo in their 400-year love/hate relationship with the Spanish, a paradox of conquering bloodshed, harsh reprisals, and extensive intermarriage. This tension shows up in a dream I had during a four-day backpacking trek through the Pecos Wilderness. I had dreamt that Robert Mirabal and a local Hispanic mountain man were out in these mountains fighting and wounding each other. Both were in considerable anguish with the pain and bloodshed they had inflected on each other. Both were wondering why this had to be. Both, at the base of their souls, had a World Two cultural perspective, but the hierarchal harshness of World Three had gotten between them.

This tension still continues between the Spanish and Native American communities. On the one hand, there is a deep connection through the irretrievable *mestizo* blend of culture and blood. On the other, shame and bitterness remains because of the historical oppression of World Two by World Three, and the later World Four hierarchy that made some Spanish ashamed of their mixed Native blood. A revitalization movement, Chicano Power (a cousin to the Black Power and American Indian Movement) turned that mestizo shame into a source of pride.

Modernizing the Goddess

Joanne Shenandoah is an acclaimed singer/songwriter of Oneida heritage. The Oneida were one of the tribes of the larger Iroquois Confederation. Like Mirabal, she too is riding the edge between Worlds, discovering the music industry as a modern vehicle to celebrate the ancient Oneida matriarchal traditions of her horticultural people. Shenandoah shared with me the unique and important force the kind of evolved consciousness this layer of culture still has to offer us:

> The clan mothers have always chosen our leaders and taken them out of office They have been responsible for the political, social, and environmental welfare of the people. Rarely have we seen a nation of women making war. The mission has been to live in harmony with one another and with nature. Every single Iroquois song is a celebration of something, whether it is animals, new life, or planting. Everything has a spirit. Because we are a matriarchal system, there are hundreds of women's songs. In every ceremony, we pay honor to women because they are our life givers.
>
> The problem around the world today is that we have a very difficult time communicating our emotions and feeling as though we have been heard and are a part of the decisions that will affect us. Traditionally, the Iroquois had a consensual

government. When there's a major decision that will affect the nation, all members of all clans get together. Everyone is then a part of a circular decision and has a mark in making that decision. This communal reality comes together most when we sing and dance. Our feet are caressing the mother earth and our voices sharing a common inner soul. This is the greatest healing force we have going or us.

Whenever we celebrate life as a group and share our blessings, the fruition of World Two is there.

Joanne Shenandoah

The problem around the world today is that we have a very difficult time communicating our emotions and feeling as though we have been heard and are a part of the decisions that will affect us.

⊛ Personal Journey
Getting Down for the Funk of It

Okay, let's try another approach. Take it back. Go past hip-hop, house, techno, and ambient rave. Keep going, through Michael Jackson and Prince and the disco wave that rock 'n' rollers put down but nevertheless revolutionized the industry. From there, travel right on by Stevie Wonder and the whole Motown phenomenon. When you land, a few crucial granddaddies of modern day funk will be left standing. These are the roots that liberated America's hips.

One of them is New Orleans, a town that never lost its original African funk because none of the town's colonizers got around to completely banning the ceremonies of the imported slaves. Fed by Caribbean populations, the oral culture of New Orleans blended syncopated island rhythms with all of what else was happening on the American mainland: work songs, spirituals, blues, European song structure and instruments, etc. Jazz was largely born out of the late 19th century funeral marches, an opportunity to celebrate one last time an improvisatory dance. One planned one's funeral by choosing the songs the band would play.

Another root was a Southern gospel converted by Atlantic Records and Stax Studios into a scorching R&B sound. Prime early ambassadors include Aretha Franklin, Wilson Pickett, and Otis Redding. This has largely been true of the gospel of the African American communities since the turn of the 20th century. The feel and drive of what was, foremost, a spiritual expression could just as easily turn out to be popular culture's next rift. Thomas Dorsey, Rosetta Tharpe, Little Richard, Sam Cooke, Franklin, James Brown (who became a funk category unto himself), and Al Green are samples of performing artists spanning the century who spent their careers jumping back and forth between gospel and secular music.

Meanwhile, on the streets of Newark, N.J. in the middle Fifties, a young wacky hairdresser by the name of George Clinton was sowing the seeds of an empire that went on to produce some of the best live shows in the history of rock' n' roll. Clinton started out innocent enough with a street-corner doo-wop sound. But soon he realized a crucial marriage was waiting, a bonding of music and motif that would put ghetto blacks and suburban brats in the same arenas. Clinton's signature song, "One Nation Under a Groove," spawned a sub-cultural social movement.

Landing full-size motherships on the stage, Clinton posed as a black hippie visiting from another planet. With an unprecedented flair, his concerts and following broke down racial barriers. Clinton manifested a clear political statement without saying anything particularly political at all. Funk became a way of life. Marrying bottom heavy urban funk with psychedelic guitar-laced rock, a pounding horn section, and all kinds of vocal prowess, a Clinton show wasn't so much a concert as a cathartic therapeutic marathon. Putting as many as thirty musicians, dancers and performers on stage, in their peak form they would play four or five hours at a time. They were the Grateful Dead of funk. Their ritual performance linked the latest and deepest of pop culture with the most ancient of ancestral wisdom and shamanic connection.

A rite of passage for me was becoming a part of that following in the late 70s. I got to know them while working in a disco kitchen in inner city Philadelphia as a young college student. We were a motley arrangement of ghetto blacks, artists, gay people, and students. While Clinton's appeal was clearly peaking then, his music made a major comeback when punk-funk stars, The Red Hot Chile Peppers, and an assortment of rappers later paid homage. Clinton was rapping before the genre existed. He shared these thoughts with me in a personal interview:

> I took what Motown had taught me, the concept of family, and applied it to funk, a midtempo between blues and rock. When Funkadelic came out, I knew it was going to take fifteen years before it caught on. The sampling really helped us. Whereas James Brown fought it, when people started playing

our stuff, I was ready to get down with them and help out with the video. Up until that point, we had never been on the radio because we were nobody's demographic. But since we had a cult following, we always just nurtured that. We are the keepers of frequency.

George Clinton

Marrying bottom heavy urban funk with psychedelic guitar-laced rock, a pounding horn section, and all kinds of vocal prowess, a Clinton show wasn't so much a concert as a cathartic therapeutic marathon.

While a product of the Black Power Era, Clinton understood that "any approach that divided the world into comfortable little categories needed rethinking" (Werner 1999). While a definitively African-American expression, Clinton was all-inclusive by his definitions of Blackness. Fittingly, cosmically, Clinton conceived of what he was doing as "funkentelechy." Entelechy means "an immanent agency that regulates or directs the vital processes of the organism" (*Merriam-Webster's Dictionary* 1967).

> Grandmaster Clinton beats the binary at its own game. Clinton most definitely plays the black pieces, although he shares James Baldwin's sense of "blackness" as an approach to life rather than a color of skin. The "white pieces" represent a frowning, judgmental, static, uptight, non-dancing, un world. In short, "reality"... Clinton's vision of funkentelechy recognizes the funk as the fundamental principle of being, the source of the form we become. Clinton refuses to respond to the either/or system in or/either terms. The white folks think Freudian; it's all about conflict, fathers chasing sons, accumulating shit, as he points out in 'Doo Doo Chasers.' The black thang's Jungian; it's about the search for integration, reconciliation with the mother and father, getting past the lines that divide the world into two. Everybody's invited on board the Mothership (a cosmic spaceship which Clinton which actually lands on stage). Doesn't mean they're going to get on board, but that's their call. (Werner, *A Change Is Gonna Come: Music, Race and the Soul of America*, 1999)

That ritual would most often involve combinations of rhythm, instrumental sound, movement, and voice. Pop musicians are simply the latest embodiment of these ancient technicians.

George Clinton described the journey (as well as the subtitle for a song) as a "psychoalphadiscobetadioaqua-doloop."

> Clinton articulates a theory of musical neurophysics or physio-neuromusicology. He weaves in references to different types of brain waves—the alpha and the beta—with mind/body references: psycho for thinking, disco for dancing. You

think and you dance and you get all of your brain operating.
Let the energies flow across the mind/body barrier and you'll
find yourself in places you didn't even know were there. It's
the key to life. And you just do it to get it over with. When you
get to the end, you do it again. Almost alone among male-led
musical groups, P-Funk plays with a feminine sexual energy. It isn't about reaching a climax and moving on; it's about
building it up, relaxing, riding the wave, climaxing, and doing it all some more. It's healing and it's fun. (Werner 1999)

This is the ritual form that grew me up. It gave me the first glimpse
of understanding the role and power of ritual throughout time. The
ritual transmission of archetypal energies is, despite all the cultural
shifts, the thread and the link from the contemporary to the most
ancient.

Rastamon Vibration

The next wave of popular culture that caught my attention
was the Rastafarian Movement. I ended up writing a Masters thesis in Anthropology about my immersion into this movement.
(The scam of my life was receiving a travel grant to go see reggae
concerts.) A 1930s Jamaican born Afro-Christian blend of politics,
religion, and ritual, Rastafari emphasizes the African input into
Biblical history. A Rastafarian, an Israelite, an Ethiopian, are synonymous identities, a cosmological union referring to a Biblical lost
tribe now found again fleeing the evils of Babylon and wandering
in the holy desert.

In 1930, the man Ras Tafari, considered to be the 111th direct
descendant of Makeda, the Queen of Sheba, and King Solomon, the
last rulers of the Israelites, was crowned Haile Selassie I, Emperor
of Ethiopia, King of Kings, Lord of Lords. Haile Selassie had no
direct involvement with the genesis of the Rastafarian movement.
He didn't have to. An ancient archetype, one connecting displaced
African peoples back to their African Christian roots, rather than an

imposed European Christianity, had been activated.

Rastafari remained a marginal movement until the mid-sixties when Rastafarian inspired musicians—many of them following the waves of Caribbean migrations to Canada, the United States, but most notably England—helped to spread its influence. By the mid-seventies, with the full emergence of reggae, Rastafari had become a global phenomenon. Through the channels of popular culture, it has become a mobile tribal expression, in short, a new world religion.

The unique achievement of reggae is in synthesizing the diverse but complimentary sounds of North American and Caribbean popular music (funk, soul, Motown, mento/calypso), sounds that have been largely derived from the New World African experience and musicianship. The actual word *reggae* is believed to be derived from a Toots and the Maytals 1967 hit "Do the Reggay." As Toot Hibbert explained, "Reggae means comin' from d'people. Regular beat the people use like food down there. We put music to it, make a dance out of it, maybe union with God if you do it right."

Whereas the roots and development of reggae included much more than the ritual practices and music of Rastafari, it was the early groups such as Marley and the Wailers, Burning Spear, Toots and the Maytals, who turned to the themes, discipline and song of Rasta, and thus gave reggae its central drive. Ironically, as an African expression, reggae first became popular in the United States among young Caucasian youth. White Rastas become the new hippies.

Why whites and not blacks? The African-American communities had a strong, spiritual celebratory root in the form of gospel. Reggae and the whole Rastafarian cosmology felt alien, especially at first, to them. However, for the White Rasta alienated from his own culture, Rastafari, via reggae, provided a sensual return to a Christian expression that had long felt hollow and condemning in his own communities. In short, Rastafari returned Christianity to its horticultural (World Two) roots. Smoking marijuana evolved from a party toy to a sanctified ritual.

In May of 1981, I flew to Montego Bay, Jamaica, to attend Bob Marley's funeral. While I have since interviewed many of the top artists of reggae—Burning Spear, Third World, Black Uhuru, Toots Hibbert, sons Ziggy and Steven Marley, Bunny Wailer—Marley was considered its founding force. Marley was part of an organization named "The Twelve Tribes of Israel" in which he was crowned Brother Joseph. It stressed as a daily discipline Selassie's urge to read a chapter of the Bible a day.

Bob Marley

Rastafari represents the fruits of World Two, a leap of consciousness from the colonially imposed brands of Christianity to an older tribal catharsis.

Aligned with other forms of Christianity, the *Bible*, when apprehended with a clean conscience and lifestyle, would supply a path, a course of action and way of thinking through the maze of civilization's unfolding. Marley was buried in a state funeral. The funeral procession began in a Kingston ceremony and then his body was driven around the island for all to witness. All schools and businesses were closed. His body finally arrived at Nine Mile, Marley's birthplace, a small village in the jungle hills of the parish of St. Ann.

There I sat on a hill of Rastas, waiting, listening to, absorbing the process of Marley's funeral broadcast all over Jamaica's ubiquitous sound system: the constant chatter of the radio commentators, the reggae interludes frequently playing Marley's acoustic "Redemption Song," the commercial breaks, the state helicopters swarming overhead. The only other visible white people were a few women who had joined Rasta clans, the people of the international press, and Edward Seaga, the prime minister of an island that is over 90 percent black.

Seaga's address was cut short. Indeed, he was ushered off the stage by what I later learned to be higher members of the Twelve Tribes. The ceremony, as has been the legacy and sustenance of the Rastafarian tradition, was completed on their own terms.

Rasta returns the temple of worship to the body and the power of group ceremony. Along the way, there are many traps. The new religion can easily be twisted to fit within the confines of the entrepreneurial paradigm. Rasta sells. New addictions (marijuana, self-righteousness) can crop up, replacing the old ones (alcohol, self-denial, self-deprecation). Rastafari represents the fruits of World Two, a leap of consciousness from the colonially imposed brands of Christianity to an older tribal catharsis.

Puebloan Dreams

I had started working on the Pueblo reservations as an applied anthropologist in the mid-1980s. My boss was a San Juan Pueblo Indian. The first day he sat down with me and looked at my resume. "So, you're an anthropologist. Don't tell anyone, and don't go sneaking around here asking a lot of nosy questions and then write it down and try to sell it. Just get to know people, and with that trust, they will share with you what they want you to know." Others have done this, journalists and anthropologists the most notable, but also Native writers, and some are now banned from setting foot in the Pueblos.

As a result, I happily shed the robes of the anthropologist, and nearly twenty years later that friendship continues. The inner journey unfolded as follows. In a dream I am having dinner with Jerome, a former student from the Taos Pueblo. He is fluent in Tiwa, their indigenous language. Jerome is known as a *kiva boy*, that is, traditionally initiated into his tribe. He spent months inside the kiva and in high mountain wilderness as part of his initiation. I first got to know him as his teacher inside a residential treatment center. His father, an alcoholic, died a couple of years previously, passed out in a snow bank. Now Jerome found himself possessed by the same spirits and need for spirits (alcohol).

In the dream, Jerome, intoxicated, suddenly stands up and is extremely upset. He is shaking and, at once, both in deep grief and deep rage. I ask him what is going on and he tells me that Spirit Eagle (who was discussed in the last chapter and whom Jerome has never met, nor had we ever talked about) has been incarcerated. His mother and I try to calm him down. I told Jerome about my dream.

While I had never been around Jerome when he has been drinking, he informed me, after telling him of this dream, that this, in fact, is exactly how he can get. A deep possessing rage wants to come out of him and my dream was picking up on this. What the dream is pointing to is the deep injustices and trauma indigenous peoples have suffered, and the anger and sadness that still needs to come out around that.

Several years later, amidst working with Pueblo clients as a psychotherapist, this next dream came to me. A young Pueblo man, striking, long black hair flowing, peers at me. Without even a twitch, bile from inside his gut forces its way outside the corner of his mouth. I interpret the dream as a man inside a bind: the deep, proud traditions of his people that contain a repressed rage that must make its way to the surface, no matter the stoic nature of his culture.

This final dream completes that thread: Mother Mary, reconfigured in Latin American Christianity as Our Lady of Guadalupe, was floating to a reggae beat. Our Lady represents the synthesized apparition of Mary and the repressed Aztec goddess, Tonantzin. To the young Mexican 16th century Native, Juan Diego, this vision of her allowed a perfect bridge and transcendence of "the tension of the opposites" between Spanish Catholic and indigenous culture.

Our Lady of Guadalupe, her visual synthesis of Marian and Native Goddess archetype, became at once the new Mary and the resurrection of the ancient Native Goddess. The dream expanded her realm further, connecting the African Caribbean experience with the Native American. Both were heavily colonized by Christianity. Both were looking for some kind of inward bridge back to their own matriarchal roots. My psyche was taking me on the journey that reconciled this vitality of World Two with the all too harsh entry of World Three to come.

Practical Applications

World Two shows up wherever the dynamics of ancient village structure are still at work. Transplanted African (Caribbean, African-American) and mestizo-forged Latino (Mexico, Central and

South American, Northern New Mexico) communities have largely operated out of the ways of World Two. These cultures came into instant conflict with the colonizing regimes of Worlds Three and Four. I've worked with these populations, as well as the Pueblo, as a teacher and counselor most of my adult life.

Most of what has been called the Third World (Asian countries, Africa, Latin America, and now Third World immigrant populations) are guided by the values of World Two. There is a strong paradox that this World must contend with. On the one hand, there is a centered, empowering consciousness fostered by group togetherness. On the other, a kind of social conformity can emerge that makes moving into the freedoms of World Four a constant bind.

The redemption of World Two culture is a kind of ritually induced catharsis that can be found in rites around the world (*i.e.*, Greek Mystery Religions, Hindu village ritual, African rhythm and song). The same cathartic principles underlie much of the drive of modern popular culture, especially the musical end. The downside is being boxed in by social conformity and/or a kind of addiction to the group high that cathartic culture entails (*i.e.*, sex, drugs and rock 'n' roll).

Much of popular music, no matter the shallow or addictive sides, hopes to keep the community feeling of World Two alive. Native peoples flock to reggae and funk, knowing these deep drum and bass driven pop rituals, the liberating expression for the transplanted African, have a healing force for them as well. I've been a pop music journalist over the course of the last twenty years. I've interviewed and seen countless "famous" musicians. I've stared their charisma in the face. World Two is alive and well in global pop culture. There is an esoteric thread (think The Beatles, Stevie Wonder, Bob Marley, Joni Mitchell, Bob Dylan) to pop music that connects us with the ancient stories and catharsis of village ritual.

For those culturally born into this World, there is a kind of power and solidarity generated here that rarely will translate into modern, industrial terms. This "high" can also be a risk, as the attempt to somehow recreate a similar high in modern terms can end up in all sorts of addictions. The challenge is to be very conscious about crossing between Worlds, and that any kind of a "spiritual high" is going to uncover wounds and traumas that the original indigenous World never had to deal with.

Assistance will most likely be needed from the techniques of other Worlds to help provide balance. There can also be within this type of culture, because of the perils of losing who one is and what one's culture has, a type of secrecy and conformity that may feel strangulating. Some of this has to do (buckle down!) with surviving the imperialism introduced by Worlds Three and Four. The response is not necessarily to buckle down more, but to find a balance between all the worlds that the Fifth World is asking for.

World Two Summary

This was that time in human history, the Neolithic Revolution (10,000 BCE), when all the shamanic elements of World One got funneled into the focused power of the group that the advent of domesticating nature (farming, pastoralism) brought to culture. Like the orchestrated flight of a flock of birds, we learned how to seamlessly move in accordance with the rhythms of nature. An empowered group healing comes about when individuals put aside their personal self-interest for the benefit of the whole.

The danger here is conformity to the group that denies individuality.

Global Archetypal Unfolding
The Neolithic Revolution

Culture's domestication of nature (farming, pastoralism) led to the unprecedented growth of villages, governmental organization, disease, and warfare.

Earth Changes

The Neolithic Revolution created an archetypal and ceremonial shift that emphasizes the needs of the group over the individual. The group's attunement was to the cycles of the agrarian year.

Mything It Out

Mythology now plays an expanded role in culture and consciousness. Pantheons of anthropomorphized Gods and Goddesses (Vedic, Greek, Roman, Celtic, Egyptian, etc.) sprout up around the world.

Mother Earth

World Two cultures, with their increased attention to the sustenance that farming creates for them, are also more attuned to matriarchal principles. The downside of this is the presence of sacrifice—animal and sometimes human—to appease the Great Mother.

The Origins of Formal Religion
World Two begins to be corrupted by its own success, leading to what is recorded in mythologies around the world as The Fall. This, in turn, leads to the scriptural development of ethical imperatives that lays the foundation for the World Religions of World Three. Sacrifice is internalized, the base parts of one's self giving way to the more exalted, selfless dimensions.

The Psychology of World Two
World Two's emphasis a group rather than individual consciousness affords a potentially greater network of support, but also an increasing social conformity to contend with.

🜂 Cultures of the Southwest—The Puebloan
The Anasazi Didn't Go Anywhere
A diverse range of groups and languages in their shift to farming culture leads to the formation of Puebloan culture, a representative embodiment of the ceremonial principles and cultural patterns of World Two.

Weather Making and Ancestral Connection
The Pueblo employment of kachina ceremony demonstrates a profound interaction with ancestral realms and weather making.

Edutainment
Pueblo professional musician Robert Mirabal embodies the connection between World Two ceremony and how these same energies and principles show up in the popular culture of the modern world.

Moderning the Goddess
Oneida singer/songwriter Joanne Shenandoah explains how the matriarchal principles of the Iroquois Confederation can still be found and encouraged in today's world.

❀ Personal Journey
Getting Down for the Funk of It
My journey into the tribal world of George Clinton and the P-Funk All Stars.

Rastamon Vibration
An account of how the Rastafarian belief system and ritual form becomes a World Religion.

🔲 Practical Applications
Therapeutic applications include any kind of group activity that supports the release and evolution of one's soul: support groups, twelve-step groups, men's groups, women's groups, attending trainings, workshops and forms of higher education, as well as ritual and communitas experiences, *i.e.*, going to concerts, group meditations, special events. It is absolutely necessary for the human condition to have our journey experienced with and reflected back by a group of us humans.

HAVE: TO HOLD OR MAINTAIN AS A POSSESSION, PRIVILEGE, OR ENTITLEMENT...HAVE-NOT: ONE THAT IS POOR ESPECIALLY IN MATERIAL WEALTH. HAVE: TO HOLD OR MAINTAIN AS A POSSESSION, PRIVILEGE, OR ENTITLEMENT...HAVE-NOT: ONE THAT IS POOR ESPECIALLY IN MATERIAL WEALTH. HAVE: TO HOLD OR MAINTAIN AS A POSSESSION, PRIVILEGE, OR ENTITLEMENT...HAVE-NOT: ONE THAT IS POOR ESPECIALLY IN MATERIAL WEALTH. HAVE: TO HOLD OR MAINTAIN AS A POSSESSION, PRIVILEGE, OR ENTITLEMENT...HAVE-NOT: ONE THAT IS POOR ESPECIALLY IN MATERIAL WEALTH. HAVE: TO HOLD OR MAINTAIN AS A POSSESSION, PRIVILEGE, OR ENTITLEMENT...HAVE-NOT: ONE THAT IS POOR ESPECIALLY IN MATERIAL WEALTH. HAVE: TO HOLD OR MAINTAIN AS A POSSESSION, PRIVILEGE, OR ENTITLEMENT...HAVE-NOT: ONE THAT IS POOR ESPECIALLY IN MATERIAL WEALTH. HAVE: TO HOLD OR MAINTAIN AS A POSSESSION, PRIVILEGE, OR ENTITLEMENT...HAVE-NOT: ONE THAT IS POOR ESPECIALLY IN MATERIAL WEALTH. HAVE: TO HOLD OR MAINTAIN AS A POSSESSION, PRIVILEGE, OR ENTITLEMENT...HAVE-NOT: ONE THAT IS POOR ESPECIALLY IN MATERIAL WEALTH. HAVE: TO HOLD OR MAINTAIN AS A POSSESSION,

THE CODEPENDENT DANCE OF THE HAVES AND HAVE-NOTS

WORLD THREE
The Rise of the World Religions

WESTERN RELIGIONS

Eastern Religions

RATIONALISM

Dependent
Co-origination

**GREEK
MYSTERY
RELIGIONS**

Bhakti

**LOGOS/
CHRIST**

Tao
Moksha

DUALISM

Yoga

---

*See the end of this chapter for further explanation of the World Three
Medicine Wheel.*

First Onset:

3500 BCE

Predominant Infrastructure:

AGRARIAN HIERARCHY

Predominant Social Structure:

EXTENDED FAMILY, FEUDALISM, NOBILITY

Predominant Superstructure:

WORLD RELIGIONS – JUDAISM / CHRISTIANITY / ISLAM /
VEDANTA HINDUISM / BUDDHISM

Predominant Medicinal Response:

WORLD MEDICAL SYSTEMS – CHINESE / AYURVEDIC / PERSIAN
/ GALENIC / PARACELSIAN

Predominant Mode of Thinking:

HIERARCHAL, CONTEMPLATIVE

Human Potential Advance:

DEEP PRAYER AND MEDITATIVE DISCIPLINES

Shadow Sides:

SOCIETAL AND RELIGIOUS IMPERIALISM

American Southwest Culture:

SPANISH

Personal Journey:

SUFI / HINDU / BUDDHIST / CHRISTIAN JOURNEY, MESTIZO
CULTURE

Global Archetypal Unfolding
History Arrives as His Story

The next world arrives swiftly and dramatically. When the smoke clears the whole social, religious and psychological landscape has changed. Once fairly egalitarian, strongly matriarchal cultures have witnessed and/or succumbed to the advent of patriarchal regimes. The small-scale horticultural world simply could not hold. Their success was their demise. Inevitably, the push and ability to grow would lead to an increasingly complex social order. The inevitable result was *hierarchy*.

This led, in turn, to a growing social injustice. Whereas we began to see the emergence of institutions in the horticultural world, in this new landscape of agrarian based hierarchy we now see institutions (*i.e.*, kingdoms, feudal structures, class/caste, the Church, the State) literally reach in and predominate people's lives. Cultures around the world became class and predominantly caste structured, producing a perennial tension between the haves and have-nots, the dominant and the dominated. This would profoundly alter the psychology of the species.

In short, in World Three, the integrity of the tribal world was breaking down. Tribal tension and warfare, both psychic and militarily, had intensified. The tribe could no longer provide the cohesion and healing that focused ritual provides. Its spirituality could be used as weaponry, what cultures worldwide referred to as "witchcraft." The Old Testament is the perfect documentation of this tribal world succumbing to chaos and strife.

Some tribal cultures around the world never hit this level of tension. There were not, in those cases, the demographic pressures and congestion to make it happen. People were too spread out.

Not so of the Nile River, of Ancient Egypt, where the first monotheisms sprouted. Not so of the Middle East, the fertile Crescent stretching from Canaan (Palestine) to the Euphrates and Tigris River valleys. Not so of the Indus River valley of India, the

Yangtze and Yellow River valleys of China. Not so of the African Kingdoms, Nubia, Kush, Axum, Mali, Ghana, Songhai, Nok, Benin, Kongo, Ndonga, Karanga. Not so of the New World's Empires, the Olmecs, Toltecs, Aztecs, Mayas, Chimus, and Incas. And then, the Greek city states and the Roman Empire would all, over time, follow suit. These were the world's first "civilizations." With all of their glories, frankly speaking, humanity has still not figured out how to manage humanely this level of power.

The priestly figures, the one-time shamans, are now cast in the mold of *prophet*, foreseeing the changes about to come. They were about to develop into humanity's first true upper class. The shifts in power came in stages. Tribal consensus leaned towards centralized leadership. This in turn led to leadership over several communities, not just one's own. Chiefs, rather than simply those naturally endowed with the abilities to facilitate consensus, evolved into broader chiefdoms whose ranks were entirely hereditary. Hierarchy emerges.

Finally full-fledged nobilities surfaced, coinciding with the rise of empire. An entrenched ruling elite had come into power and would forever be reluctant to let go of the reins. The formation of the State, and all of its bureaucratic enforcement, would guarantee that.

The textures would vary in cultures around the world, but the underlying shift that World Three produced was the same: momentous growth of villages into towns and cities, the emergence of crime and civil distrust, the invention and enforcement of law to assure order, the dramatic rise of slavery alongside kill and conquering warfare, the unprecedented intermixture of race and culture, the invention of writing, metallurgy, and more sophisticated mathematical and calendar systems.

While the first cities reach back to around 8,000 BCE, agrarian hierarchal societies began to dominate globally around 4,000 to 2,000 BCE. The first great military empires, be it "the Alexanders and Caesars and Sargons and Khans" (Ken Wilber, *Up from Eden*,

1996) would, by 3000 BCE, begin to colonize the planet.

According to Hindu chronology, this date marks the arrival of the *Kali Yuga*, the final and most decadent of humanity, the Age of Conflicts:

> Men's senses are disturbed by darkness and they fall prey to illusion and jealousy... In the Dark Age, drought pits one country against another. Scripture has no authority, and men take to the violation of dharma (duty, path); they act without dharma, without morality, they are very angry and not very smart... When scripture is destroyed, then people will kill one another, for they will have no moral boundaries, no check to their violence, no affection, and no shame. (Fieser, *Scriptures of the East*, 2004)

The good news, the resolution the world religions pursue, is also tracked out by the Kali Yuga:

> From this numbness there will arise thought, and thought makes the mind balanced. Understanding comes from a balanced mind, and from understanding comes a dedication to dharma. The people who are left at the end of the Dark Age will have a kind of formless mental peace. (Fieser 2004)

Out of the alienation that hierarchy creates, so comes the commitment to an even deeper freedom.

Divine Kingship

In the form of nobilities, from China and India across the Middle East and Greece to the New World, many of these new hierarchies believed in and tried to uphold the principles of "divine kingship." The ruler was to be a mere vehicle for God's work, a divine servant of the people. It is hard to gage in retrospect how successful this ever was, as history more glaringly shows off the rampant examples of absolute power corrupting absolutely. This kind of God-ordered hierarchy becomes known as *theocracy*, and was supported by an ecclesiastic chain of command. The Vatican is a modern day example of this ancient structure.

I had a dream when Bill Clinton first became president in 1992, amidst a wave of great liberal optimism. In the dream, Clinton was pondering whether a President could truly serve the will of the people. The President noted, "This is how it used to be with our divine kings." The dream indicated to me that alignment and surrender to a higher power was a possibility even amidst steep hierarchy and tremendous centralizing of power.

The advent of democracy, a primary World Four motif, doesn't necessarily enhance that. If the political and economic leaders have not learned how to truly manage their position of power towards a higher good, it really doesn't matter what the governmental form is. Greed takes over. That's where (and why) the world religions come into the picture.

In World Three, at first, the polytheistic expressions of World Two are translated into hierarchal pantheons of Gods and Goddesses. This is how the ancient worlds of Egypt, India, Greece, the Maya, the Aztec and the northern Germanic and Scandinavian tribes looked, with figures such as, respectively, Ra, Rudra (who would meld into Shiva), Zeus, Kulkulkan, Quetzalcoatl, Wotan and Thor, perched at the highest command center. But with the increasing colonization of diverse peoples something had to budge.

A larger umbrella belief system and deeper metaphysic had to be developed. Expanding populations combined with the increasing prevalence that those divine kingships could turn out to be not so divine and rather cruel. A new consciousness, and reach for consciousness, was about to be born. Suffering, as is its evolutionary nature, demanded a way out.

The Hero in a New World

The individual, whose self-definition was once filled in and bolstered by clan and tribe, now faces an uncaring, coercive society. Not having the support of the group to fall back onto, a new kind of hero was needed. The hero needed somehow be able to atone for the feelings of anguished self-responsibility that beset him. As the pioneer explorer of consciousness, Jean Houston noticed in the early scripture of these dawning World Religions:

> The hero could not just be a lonely adventurer. After a while he could not stand himself, for he could not live without values, standards, patterns of prestige. He had to have some code of honor, some new forms of commonality. In the Sanskrit "Mahabharata" and "Ramayana," in much of Genesis, in book of Judges, Samuels, and 1 Kings, in the Iliad and the Odyssey, in the Icelandic Eddas, and in many other epics and sagas of the heroic age, we find the same phenomenon: warriors (heroes) easily shamed and driven to a code of standards. List of thou-shalt-nots, tabulation of censures, and the exhortation to noble acts—these are the patterns that form the moral background of epic literature. (Houston, *Life-Force: The Psycho-Historical Recovery of the Self*, 1993)

The hero needed a more precise blueprint, an ethical standard, to live by. These were also the first published forms of the personal pronoun *I*. The modern sense of the isolated self was born hand in hand with the attempts to move out of that isolation. The ego seeks to resolve the anguish it produces.

The push forward was a paradoxical one. Societies, as a whole, now started incorporating these ethical standards; societies sustained by hierarchal regimes that were hardly ethical at all. The Ten Commandments is the most prominent example. These standards were not, at first, about keeping people in line, but more asking individuals to be responsible, since society was not. What are we doing with our energy, to others, to ourselves?

As a consequence, a more obedient, transcendent state of consciousness was needed. In response, sages from around the world—Plato, Gautama Buddha, Socrates, Parmenides, Confucius, Patanjali, the holy ones of the *Upanishads*—began to speak out. This has come to be known as existentialist philosopher Karl Jaspers termed it, "the axial age of history," a planetary need for a deeper wisdom, both societal and personal. These sages would give us the recipes to help these heroes—that is, the archetypal role models for us everyday people—to survive in a world that had grown all too harsh.

Birth of the World Religions

The philosophical and spiritual genius of India and Greece led the way for the globe's respective Eastern and Western hemispheres. Ancient Greece would then exchange wisdom with the sensibilities of Middle Eastern culture, most notably Egyptian and Persian, and finally assimilate the "paradigm busting" journey of a small tribe known as the Hebrews. The result was the Judeo-Christian lineage. Islam would later add to this, which altogether became known as the Abrahamic faiths. When the dust settled, these faiths become the greatest force the planet had ever known, although often oddly at odds both with itself and the planet's other wisdom traditions.

Meanwhile the religious advances of India began to travel and combine with the traditions of China (Taoism, Confucianism) and other indigenous expressions (*i.e.,* Shinto). This Hindu-Buddhist lineage would pervade much of the East and, in modern times, completely fascinate the West. East and West, however, have always been connected. Central Asia has always allowed for crossroads of culture. The ancient lineage of Sufism, Sikhism's 16th century integration of Islam and Hindu principles, and the industrial world's propensity to mix and match religions, are continuing examples of this East-West synthesis.

These new broader belief systems, monotheistic in the Middle East, more *monistic* (a search for and surrender to Oneness) in the East, develop so as to resolve the tribal tensions this new world of hierarchy contained. The West concentrated on salvation, the East liberation, but it was the same social upheaval these systems were responding to. The tribe was no longer around to take care of everyone's needs. People began to fall through the cracks of these new hierarchal societies. Consciousness, once gathered in the clan and the tribe, is concentrated more and more so within the individual. The world now can truly become a lonely place.

These new religions—Judaism, Christianity, Islam, Hinduism, Buddhism—promise and provide a kind of transcendent redemption beyond this lack of social solidarity. Unfortunately, these religions were also pulled in by and began representing the very regimes they were originally critiquing. You got it coming and going.

Loss of the Feminine

This is how World Three shows up in the Middle East, the crucible of Western culture:

> One city or another would from time to time extend military control over its neighbors, forming a larger political unit, and exalt its main deity over those of its subjects. Occasionally, one such city would rise to the status of empire, with wide influence over its geographical area, imposing its god on many subcultures and subsuming the qualities of other gods into its own. This was the genesis and mechanism of the rise of monotheism, achieved first in Mesopotamia, Persia, and Greece. (Riley, *One Jesus, Many Christs*, 1997)

Thus the Biblical declaration, "You shall have no other gods before me." The monistic tendency of the East would unfold differently, much more tolerant of religious diversity, but it is still the politics of a patriarchal hierarchy, known as "state bureaucracy"—be it in the Hindu Laws of Manu, the messianic zeal of Ashoka's North Indian Buddhist kingdom, Tibetan theocracy, or China's Confucian driven feudal empires—that was calling the shots.

The consequences are profound. These new hierarchies would eliminate ninety percent of the world's female deities. The older polytheisms would be destroyed and/or absorbed by a variety of strategies. In the West, many of the same polytheistic figures would turn up as saints, and the variety of Goddess figures would all eventually be funneled down to some version of the Virgin Mary. Virgin births, after all, were already well depicted in myths worldwide.

According to Marija Gimbutas and other like-minded archeologists, the beginning of the end started around 4500 BCE when fierce horsemen swept down from the steppes of Asia. Mother earth cultures were conquered and replaced by a hierarchal system ruled by sky gods. There is no doubt truth to all of this, the places of worship shifting from caves and structures burrowed into the mother earth to pyramids and edifices reaching to the father sky, the Father God.

The more significant transformation, however, was occurring within. The creation of private property and hoarding of surplus wealth was the outer realm of this birthing hierarchal world. As Leonard Shlain tracks in his work *The Alphabet and the Goddess*, these were all results of another more primary shift:

> Image turned into cuneiform, which turned into alphabet and eventually into law. It was not the barbaric warrior who killed the goddess. It was the first bureaucrat. The Scribes transferred the authority previously vested in the shaman's chanted spells to the written word. Now, abstraction called a law was in effect even when no one of influence was present. Posted throughout the kingdom on stone stelae, these abstractions took on a life of their own, outliving the lawmakers themselves. (Shlain 1998)

Societal law had replaced natural law.

Written language, while certainly flowering into all kinds of poetic possibilities, nevertheless, began as a way to keep tabs on the masses. Simultaneously, by the linear, grammatical nature of its own composition, literacy—which for much of human history was confined to the ruling and priestly classes—tended to throw people into their analytical *left brain* as opposed to the more holistic, intuitively oriented *right brain*. The feminine was losing out on all fronts.

The historical and spiritual movements this shift into patriarchy that World Three introduces is entirely too complex to trace in this work. There are, however, two prominent lineages that indicate the evolution in consciousness needed to address this cultural change. There are very few on the planet that have not, in some manner, been affected by these lineages.

The one, the Abrahamic faiths lineage, accounts for the two largest religions currently on the planet, Christianity and Islam, though they have their origin in a small Middle Eastern tribe known as the Hebrews. The other, the Hindu-Jain-Buddhist continuum, provides some of the most advanced metaphysical explorations humanity has ever known. This evolution is where the rest of this chapter will concentrate.

The Abrahamic Faiths

From the lens of a mythic storytelling, a quick run through of the Abrahamic lineage looks something like this. As a reflection of society's increasing violence, Zoroaster, the prophet of Persia approximately 1,000 years before Christ, worships Lord Mazda, one of the world's first pronounced monotheistic deities. He also decides to declare a holy war against the *daevas*, the former nature spirits that now seem to have a more volatile, threatening characteristic. Similarly, the Greek word, *daimones*, originally meaning divinity, also becomes the root for demonic.

The spirit world could no longer be trusted. A greater benevolent and omnipotent deity had to be turned to in order to transcend what had become the harsh realities of good and evil. This dualism then later becomes readily imported into Hebrew cosmology, the evil side of which becomes the figure we now know as Satan.

Adopted by the faith of the neighboring Israelites after the Babylonian exile (586 BCE), this sharp dualism describes a world in which the Hebrew's indigenous spirit forces (*eloahim*) were transferred into a monotheistic entity. *Yahweh* was a stern god among their pantheon of gods, much like Zeus, Wotan, Thor and Shiva. The Hebrews, however, turned to him as their One God, clearly beckoning for and inviting a greater, protective and benevolent force to stand up to a world of darkness. The dualism makes sense, a reflection of a torn society in which the hopes of a cohesive, tribal religion had broken down into a corrupt and violent tribalism.

The consequences, however, would be just as violent. The Abrahamic faiths would draw definitive lines on how much they would accept of other tribal ways from around the world. The spiritual breakdown in the Middle East gets projected, without a whole lot of discernment, on to indigenous people everywhere. These faiths were blinded by their own paradigm.

Meanwhile, the vision of a Jewish nation did not come to be. Instead, the Vision comes increasingly transmitted as "The Word" through small gatherings led by teachers known as *rabbis*. One's knowledge could profoundly determine one's destiny. An unprecedented self-responsibility was being asked of the individual. Consciousness would forever be changed.

The Jewish people, however, continued to suffer. It is onto this historical stage that Jesus was born, a world in which two-thirds of the populace was encumbered by some type of slavery and servitude. The Devil felt very real. It was no wonder that Jesus was cast into the role of the classic hero in a battle with the forces of darkness. While clearly evident in society, this same battle became entrenched within. Internalized oppression was the psychology of the day.

The Jews hope for a messiah to lead them out of their desolation and, sure enough, one shows up. He insists that the Kingdom is within, and predictably the kingdom doesn't go for it. His persecution and death only empowers his metaphors. The Christ is here now. All one has to do is turn everything over to him.

Indigenous culture (Worlds One and Two) handles the terror of life and death, of time, by supporting a circular, regenerative concept of time. Everything returns on itself, including the dance of life and death. But World Three tears that circle open and much of what is left is the terror of an open ended, linear time with no resolution.

Culturally and psychologically, there was no safety net. The Christ slices through this. In surrender to the Christ, a peace-filled consciousness is offered. The question remains whether mythic structure gets swept away with the advent of historical time and the Christ resolution, or does the Christ simply build upon the older body of myth?

What seems clear is that on the level of popular culture, that is how most people are living their lives, the psyche is responding in characteristically mythic ways.

All were locked in the cosmic drama: the role of the suffering but righteous individual, of the hero, was to be lived by everyone regardless of social class. The mighty struggles with fate and injustice and the dark powers became the struggles that all were asked to face: "Take up your cross and follow me." The short and difficult lives of those who heard him were such because that was how the very universe was structured: the poor were blessed not as objects of pity or charity but as central players in the cosmic drama. For those who would follow Jesus, this gave unprecedented value to the life of even the basest individual. The rich and powerful were in real danger, for in his words, "What does it profit to gain the whole world and lose one's soul." Now the blessed afterlife, the eternal reward for perseverance and integrity, was opened as heaven to all, but especially to the poor. (Riley 1997)

Such was the perfect antidote to this harsh, hierarchal world.

While there was historical uncertainty about who Jesus really was, it was clear that he stepped into and fully embodied a new kind of archetype. Life was no longer about the fate of the Gods, one's allotment in society, or even one's bravado. Life was about striving for and maintaining certain ethical standards and surrendering everything else—one's hardship, one's suffering—to the God within. The Christ would take care of the rest.

The God Within

The notion of a "God within," however, did not start with Jesus Christ. In the 500 years before Christ, the West's Mystery Religions, operated similarly. Their rituals (Dionysian, Eleusian) were largely known via Greek culture, but because of the Mediterranean's fluid cultural exchange, the Mystery Religions represented the culmination of a potpourri of Middle Eastern and Greek cultures. For instance, one of the more prominent messengers, the Greek God Hermes, was also readily identifiable as the Egyptian deity Thoth.

These rituals would later fill in the core—the Eucharist, Baptism, Communion—of Christianity's ceremonial form. Persephone and Demeter, Orpheus and Eurydice, the pairing of God and Goddess mythological figures, were the theatrical vehicles by which to ritually enter into and cathartically cleanse oneself of one's suffering. Another figure, Dionysus, would become darn near Christlike in people's willingness to surrender their lives to the ecstasy the rituals for him provoked.

As Karen Armstrong astutely unveils in her unfolding of the Axial Age,

> The whole group fell into a trance, a heightened state of consciousness, which spread from one celebrant to another. When this happened, worshippers knew that Dionysus was present among them. They called this experience of divine possession "entheos: within a god." (Armstrong, *The Great Transformation*, 2007)

Even as the Greeks became more rational and societal in their response to life's dilemmas—the birthing of the modern republic—they could not purge popular culture of this thirst for ritual transcendence.

Christianity succeeds by bridging the mythical matrix of the older Mediterranean horticultural world with its own monotheistic, ethical imperatives. Indeed, it is out of these mystery cults where most of the symbolism of the Eucharist is derived.

> Mystery cults were old in the culture and became quite influential by the time of the Roman Empire. Originally, they had to do mainly with Demeter, the grain goddess, and Dionysus, the god of wine and inspiration, though a number of other smaller cults existed. They were so successful in providing hope and meaning to their adherents that eventually all cults borrowed at least some of their characteristics. They were not exclusive cults; members were often initiated into more than one. They were syncretistic; that is they melded and borrowed ideas and rituals from one another, identifying their gods with those of other cults. (Riley 1997)

The Christ builds off of the "ecstatic foundations" of the mix of indigenous Mediterranean culture.

The Greek term *logos*—the order of things—gets translated as The Word in the Bible, but stands for so much more. Combined with the Dionysian ritual form, much of Christianity's foundation is set:

> While the early Christians personified the Logos in the figure of Jesus, the Greeks had represented the Logos in the figure of Apollo, the god of geometry and music…. Another favorite representation was Hermes (identified in Egyptian culture as Thoth), who, as the church fathers acknowledge, was actually called "the Logos" by the Greeks. The Greek Hermetic writings, the ideas of this "pagan gnosticism" were certainly in the air during the formative days of early Christianity, and it seems clear that the person who wrote the Gospel of John was working with similar presuppositions and along similar

lines to those of the Hermetic authors.... Like the teachings of the early Christians, the Hermetic writings focus upon the mystery of the soul's rebirth and transfiguration, the discovery of "the inner man," which results in a divinization of the personality. (Fideler, *Jesus Christ, Sun of God*, 1993)

A Christ Consciousness, building off of the mythical heroes of previous ages, was being birthed. Christ was the culmination of an evolutionary process that the individual could know God—the totality of being human—from within. The cultural heroes, from the mythical Apollo to Hermes to Dionysus, and then fully embodied in a real man history has called Jesus (*Yeshua* in his own Aramaic language), were our archetypal guides.

Will the Real Jesus Please Stand Up

Because of Jesus' renown as a healer, he sometimes became confused with Asclepius, one of the most popular Roman Gods from the 4th century BCE to the 4th century CE, and to whom hundreds of healing centers were built. As expressed in the second century CE, "When we say that Jesus healed the lame and the paralytics and those ill from birth and raised the dead, we seem to be saying the same things said to have been done by Asclepius" (Riley 1997).

This is in no way an effort to downplay the authenticity of Jesus the Christ. To the contrary, even though there was historical confusion over who this individual was, there was an unprecedented sway Jesus was having on the *inner plane* of the hearts and minds of a tremendous culturally diverse range of people. The power of the Christ archetype was the ability to travel and assimilate local folkloric and mythic archetypal features wherever it went. The exalted healer archetype was already well sought and activated in the psyche of the common individual. Jesus came along to fully fill out that terrain.

Over time, Jesus the Christ becomes a man of many different cultures, faces, and races. As the Bible itself is the compendium of stories, so are the cultural montages that came to be called Jesus the Messiah. He shows up in pictures looking Oriental, Ethiopian, Semitic, African, etc., as cultures place their own face on this new hero and consciousness. This improvised, sacred synthesis of archetypes at work here—the lover, the warrior, the protector, the teacher, the healer, and the sage—culminates with the supreme archetype, the King. This makes perfect anthropological sense as monarchies are the order of the day. It is to be the Kingdom of God that integrates all of these archetypes.

Inevitably, the Christians become institutionalized, pulled into a governing role in the very hierarchy they had been persecuted by:

> There were no orthodox or heretics in the beginning—the first Christians did not originally know quite what to think of Jesus beyond the fact that he was their hero and leader and that they should follow him as best they could to the death. They started with a wide variety of ideas in their attempts to explain his career and person, often quite contradictory, drawn from the various possibilities already present in their culture and experience. (Riley 1997)

The *facts* of Jesus were not nearly as important as the *myth* of Jesus. This is how myth works. It always has. Myth sways the psyche towards its own inner *wholeness* (holiness).

Gnosticism

Gnosis means to know thyself. Forms of Western Gnosticism certainly preceded Christianity, and all Christian denominations are in their essence Gnostic. To know Christ is to know the true self. However, the term became a way of distinguishing Christianity's emerging ecclesiastic hierarchy from those "outside of the fold."

Largely flourishing in Asia Minor and Egypt, Gnosticism was then not a Church *per se*, but rather a groundswell of spiritual beliefs and practices that exhibited less institutionalized, more individualized paths to the Christ. Aspiring to an esoteric inner knowing, any form of a Church was seen as a scaffold to be torn away as the Christ was being reached.

Gnosticism also reached back towards a pre-patriarchal foundation, a kind of yin-yang take on Western cosmologies. The consort for Christ was not the Father, but the feminine, Sophia, the ancient Goddess of wisdom. Much like the Tibetan pairing of Upaya and Prajnaparamta, the masculine was about the cutting edge discernment on how to function wisely in the world, the feminine the deep reservoir of wisdom and repose the masculine draws from and returns to. From the Gnostic *Great Announcement:*

> From the power of silence appeared a great power, the Mind of the Universe, which manages all things, and is a male, the other a Great Intelligence is a female which produces all things.... There is in everyone divine power existing in a latent condition. This is power divided above and below; generating itself, making itself grow, seeking itself, finding itself, being mother of itself, father of itself, sister of itself, spouse of itself, daughter of itself, son of itself—mother, father, unity, being a source of the entire circle of existence. (Pagels, *The Gnostic Gospels*, 1979)

Gnostic cosmology was the bridge from the androgynous core of Worlds One and Two to the Christ of World Three. The hierarchy of the Church, being birthed in the second century after Jesus' passing, would begin to tear away at that bridge.

In the year 185 CE, Gnosticism was already under intense scrutiny. By 200 CE, virtually all the feminine imagery for God had disappeared from what was becoming a fairly singular Christian way of seeing the world. It was not that the resulting institutionalized Christianity was somehow less Gnostic, as the religion was still about the quest to know and redeem thyself through the Christ. It is that the institution of the Church dictated more and more how the individual was to do that.

Institutional Coercion

The major gap between Eastern and Western religion occurs right here. Because of increasing societal limitations, the diverse spread of esoteric Christianity in the West largely goes underground or disappears altogether.

> The bishops drew the line against those who challenged any of the three elements of their system: doctrine, ritual, and clerical hierarchy—and the Gnostics challenged them all. Only by suppressing Gnosticism did orthodox leaders establish that system of organization which united all believers into a single institutional structure.... There was no toleration for any who claimed exemption from doctrinal conformity, from ritual participation, and from obedience to the discipline that priests and bishops administered. Gnostic churches, which rejected that system for more subjective forms of religious affiliation, survived, as churches, for only a few hundred years. (Pagels 1979)

By 313 CE, the year Emperor Constantine adopted Christianity as the state religion, and 325 CE, the formation of the Nicean Creed, it was a done deal. The Christians, once themselves severely persecuted groups of "pagan" outsiders, in their first move as new rulers of the hierarchy turned around and persecuted the Gnostics. What goes around comes around: the oppressed becomes the oppressor.

This distinction between Gnostic and non-Gnostic actually seems to be a solid case of historical revisionism. For the first three centuries, Christianity was composed of a wide and diverse array of sects and practices. Not until the faith called Catholicism became a dominating hierarchy did there then appear those expressions that were in opposition to it. But the fact is, that as Cynthia Bourgeault shares in her work (*The Wisdom Jesus*, 2008), Roman based Christianity only forms 90 degrees of the 360-degree sweep by which this new faith spreads beyond its Middle Eastern origins, the Ethiopian and Oriental Orthodox denominations being the primary examples. Again, a more accurate way of describing Gnosticism, as no churches were overtly wearing this banner, were simply those following that fell "outside of the Roman fold."

With this said, from the 4th century forward, Christianity would the sanctifying force for European imperialism, both at home and abroad. In a strange twist, Christianity, the religion of the sufferer, becomes the colonizing tool of the oppressor. Ironically, this all seems as part of an even larger divine plan. Who better than the oppressed to identify with the role of Christ the sufferer?

The people on the oppressed and colonized end of this did their best to appropriate this imposed religion on their own terms. "The white man (he said) goes into his church and talks about Jesus, but the Indian goes into his tipi and talks to Jesus," noted Quannah Parker, Plains Indian Peyote Shaman (Mooney 1991). The African-American populations would create a similar synthesis, converting the religion of the enslavers into one of personal and societal (civil rights) liberation.

While most of the cathartic, sensuous aspects of the Christian ritual were abolished by the Inquisition (as discussed in World Four), all of this returned many fold with a series of America's "revivalist awakenings" that have stretched from the 18th to the current century. Most moving was a New World African Christian praise and worship experience that put the "funk" back into a religion largely stripped of its original healing form and intent. Jesus was the human born to fully step into the Christ, but each conquered culture experienced and expressed this sacred archetype as they culturally saw fit.

Theocratic Order

Six centuries after Christ, Mohammad goes into a cave, illiterate and beckoning towards the same Abrahamic God. He is concerned for the spiritual and societal breakdown of his Bedouin tribal peoples. This is a poor population living on the Arabic peninsula whose needs are unattended by the more urbanized Jews and Christians.

Mohammad channels what becomes the Quran, of which 80 percent of the stories are linked to the Old and New Testaments. There is not a whole lot new under the sun. To some measure, he attempts reconciliation with his Abrahamic Jewish and Christian brethren, but it doesn't happen. Turning the direction of prayer from Jerusalem to Mecca foreshadows decades of tension and conflict to come.

Islam begins out of the same exact worldly circumstances as its Abrahamic predecessors: the corruption of the tribal world, spirituality turned into a weapon, and the coincident arising of a harsh and unjust hierarchal world. A greater justice, both within and without, is called for.

Mohammad takes the Abrahamic vision to its logical conclusion: a theocratic ordering. The cleric would serve as both governmental and spiritual leader. Islam becomes the theocratic nation(s) that the Jews had always longed to be.

Starting back in the 7th century, who are to be considered the rightful leaders accounts for the Sunni/Sh'ite split. That division, along with the threat of consumer culture that World Four introduces, readily explains the schism now plaguing the Islamic/Western worlds. From the Islamic point of view, gaining democracy, which seems to go hand in hand with consumerism, necessarily risks losing one's moral order and theocratic point of view.

In World Three, theocracies soon covered the globe. A bold and binding force, monarchs posed as divine representatives, but in many a ruthless, feudal dictator, proved to be all too human. Tibet would be the sterling exception. Transformed from a nation of feuding warlords, they would go a thousand years without war. Unprecedented. Unrepeated. Overall, however, Tibetan theocracy would also be plagued by hierarchal constriction and abuse. This is the way of World Three, of empire, and humanity still hasn't recovered. How well we are able to hold the centralized power of a stratified world in a balanced way just may remain our most pressing challenge. The Dalai Lama recognized this, which is why at first he was willing to consider Mao Zedong's Communist experiment. However, when the Chinese leader, in a personal meeting with the young Dalai Lama, spoke of religion as a whore, the Tibetan leader knew that relinquishing his nation's Buddhist heart was tantamount to throwing the baby out with the bathwater. The current Dalai Lama is the incarnated embodiment of this special transmission. How well we are able to hold the centralized power of a stratified world in a balanced, just way remains the burning challenge for Worlds Three and Four.

The Journey of the East

Be it God and salvation in the West or Oneness and liberation in the East, the common people still most closely related to human-like deity figures, the heroes. In the East, however, *henotheism* would prevail; the belief that any one God or Goddess stands for the "One God" beyond all names:

In our Hindu religion, we worship God in some form. God is infinite, but we cannot imagine the infinite. We must have some finite person—whom I love like a friend, like father, like son, like lover. We make a relation with God like this. When I think he is my lover, I can always think of him. When I think he is my father, when I am in trouble, I pray to him, ask him to save me. And I always pray to the Holy Mother...I feel something. Somebody is standing behind me. I feel always the hands on my shoulders, guarding me. A mother wants nothing from a child but love. She says only, "Pray to me, call me, and I will do everything for you." While I want everything from God, God does not want anything from me except *bhatkti*—devotion. (Interview with Sarala Chakrabarty, a Calcutta grandmother in Fisher, *Living Religions*, 2002)

Remarkably, there was not competition, but rather mutual respect between the numerous deity figures. Any one deity stands for the one almighty God.

Henceforth, the East would do a much better job of tolerating and incorporating its polytheistic, shamanic beginnings. Hinduism, which was not formally termed such until the 19th century entry of the British, began as the shamanic yogic practices of the Dravidian peoples (genetically related to Australia's aborigines) that then melded into the patriarchal social structures of the invading Aryans. To what extent this coming together of disparate populations was a conquering or a synthesis is still a modern academic debate.

The irony is that whereas Eastern and Western religions would seem to be culturally removed from each other, they fed off a common thread. Originally based out of Russia's southern steppes, a widespread amorphous Aryan population had split into two, one drifting into Europe—Scandinavia, Germany, Italy, Greece—the other migrating through Persia, and then later on to what is modern day Afghanistan, the Punjab of Western India and the Hindus River Valley. Thus, the conglomerate term Indo-European (and why centuries later Adolph Hitler and his Germanic following would tragically adopt the Eastern swastika as indicative of their "pure Aryan origins"). The Western Latin and Eastern Sanskrit were linguistic cousins.

The *Vedas* (1500-600 BCE) are considered to be the planet's oldest scripture in written form. The major shift that happened was this. The Aryan tribes arrived into what was already a mightily developed civilization by 2300 BCE, "an ancient Indian empire that had been larger than either Egypt or Mesopotamia." (Armstrong

2007.) While considered the foundation of the Eastern religion Hinduism, linguistically and culturally the Vedas were a complex mix of Western and Eastern influences.

A collection of poetic praises, the Vedas portray nature spirits, known as *devas* or the shining ones, as submitting to a higher order, *rita*, which is the Sanskrit parallel to the English word *rite*. As the enunciators of the actual sacred syllables of these stanzas, a new social grouping emerged. Known as *rishis* or seers, they developed meditative techniques by which the impurities of the phenomenal world could be burned away to a greater, more exalted reality. Thus, the significance of *agni* (related to the English word to *ignite*), the spirit of fire that burns away all that is extraneous.

Ironically, the very freedom this suggests becomes coupled with a restrictive social caste that lumps many of these seers into the priestly order of Brahmins. Along with the warrior caste, they begin to govern over craftsmen, peasants and those considered outcast, known also as the *untouchables*.

Buddhism (the first Buddhist Council—480 BCE) then becomes a reformed and refined Hinduism, critiquing its ritual excesses and caste injustices. Buddhism becomes a kind of individualized, investigative psychology. It cleverly dodges the more obvious spiritual issues (*i.e.*, the existence of God), implicitly knowing that, no matter what, religions are going to turn these into a political football. Instead, Buddhism insists we discover the truths of existence for ourselves, and get in touch with and cleanse ourselves of the elements that cloud our perception. *Nirvana* means to "blow out," to extinguish that which is in our way of true evolution.

As a part of Asia's respective social structures, however, Buddhism would continue to perpetuate many of the same patriarchal ways. In theory, but rarely in practice, were women accepted as equals. Hinduism, mindful of Buddhism's critiques, introduces the less ritually encumbered Vedanta schools of philosophy so as to keep pace with Buddhism's social critique and leap in consciousness.

Quintessentially, Hinduism, Buddhism, and the lesser known Jainism, were built off of the same principles—the evolution of the soul from misplaced *karma* (deeds) and the use of meditative techniques promoting non-harming (*ahimsa*) to oneself and others. The aim is an increasing break from the cycles of birth/death/rebirth (*samsara*), a liberation—*moksha, samadhi, nirvana, satori*—that are our psychic inheritance.

However, wherever these Eastern religions traveled, whatever their principles may have been, in reality they took their polytheistic roots with them. We humans like human form. As much as the historical Buddha admonished against the practice, we couldn't help but make statues of and worship him.

Most of the East evolved into some kind of feudalistic form, but these new World Religions – Taoism, Jainism, Hinduism, Buddhism – took off some of the hierarchal edge. Personal liberation, from the social structure, from the constraints of self, was the ultimate goal. Empire, however, was still the order of the day.

When the Western World Religion Islam migrated East at the end of the last millennium (950 CE), another perennial conflict—Hindu/Muslim—was born. For all their professed wisdom, in reality the World Religions had a hard time getting along. This speaks, I suggest, to the un-evolved nature of humanity, not the spiritual principles of these religions.

Eastern Religions, however, wherever they took residence continued to readily absorb and synthesize the shamanic foundation of those respective cultures. In pre-Mao China or current day Japan, it has not at all been uncommon to see East Indian tantric deities, Taoist motifs, Shinto rituals, and Buddhist practices, all wrapped up in one dazzling bundle. The Western Religions would not be so tolerant.

Where East Meets West

This is what we have found out. Both West and East struggled with the ever-increasing advent of unjust social realities. However, the West tends to turn this into a cosmological battle of good versus evil, while the East attempts to meditatively undermine its essential existence. Either way, a repressive caste-ordered society takes over, although the later commentaries on the Vedas would give East Indian society permission to walk away from it.

Known as *saddhus* or holy ones, this East Indian rite of passage is terribly unique. One goes through the rites of responsible householder and citizen only to finally denounce it as the *essential illusion* that societal life is. *Brahman*, once merely a divine mantra, poses as an overseeing unitary concept much in the way Mazda and the later Abrahamic central deities (Yahweh, Allah) will.

Atman, the individual soul, becomes the microcosmic vehicle by which we are to know this greater world soul, Brahman. Thus, Atman/Brahman captures the notion of the wholeness of the world soul that is within us. Ultimately, this distinction between the personal soul and the world soul, the Atman/Brahman, is superfluous. This explains why they are punctuated as One.

The Christ, as the embodiment of God, is not suggesting much different, although clearly this unitary experience is personally mediated through the archetype and individual known as Jesus. A more personalized and human like relationship with God is developed. This makes sense in that 500 years has passed since the Upanishads, the last major commentary on the Vedas. The Western stratified social order had grown even harsher. People needed to feel God really close.

The cold realities of World Three demanded a more personalized, humanized redemptive force. Jesus the Christ arrives. But whether it is Atman/Brahman or Christ/God, the implications are the same. The struggles of the world reflect our own, our struggles reflect those of the world.

The consciousness advance is what the East would call *ahimsa* (non-harming), the West, *love*. Ahimsa breaks the cycle of misdeeds and violence, which Gandhi, centuries later would apply to *take down* the British Empire. It is no coincidence that Martin Luther King spent a month in India studying *ahimsa* as a complement to his own Christian faith.

This understanding helped him form the philosophical foundation of the civil rights non-violent, civil disobedience tactics. Psychologically and socially, there is a considerable feat being asked, an opening of one's heart in hell. Violence and hatred were to be met and conquered by love.

Carl Jung, independently and in his own fashion, would create a psychology based on a similar microcosmic-macrocosmic notion. The melding of the personal Soul into the World Soul, of Atman into Brahman, of Christ into the Father God, in Jung's scenario becomes the surrendering of the Ego to the Self. Jung states,

> Not through me alone, but through all; for it is not only the individual Atman but Atman/Brahman, the universal Atman, the pneuma, who breathes through all. We use the word "Self" for this, contrasting it with the little ego. From what I have said it will be clear that this Self is not just a rather more conscious or intensified ego, as the words "self-conscious," "self-satisfied," etc. might lead to one suppose. What is meant by the Self is not only in me but in all beings, like the Atman, like Tao. It is psychic totality. (Jung in Coward, *Jung and Eastern Thought*, 1985)

Consciousness itself, once inseparably interconnected with the social order, now beckons for its own enlightened wholeness. This is a momentous shift.

This is not to lump Eastern and Western religions into one category. Each must be understood by the cultural context from which they emerged. However, what is universal is: 1) an individualized ethical imperative in societies that have become all too unethical, 2) a psychology that asks that we ruthlessly take inventory of our-

selves, and 3) a metaphysics suggesting that beneath and propelling our evolutionary journey (however difficult) are principles and
practices that lead to an intrinsic wholeness.

Thus, the Buddhist lay precepts—no stealing, no lying, no killing, no intoxication, and no sexual misconduct—are nearly identical
to what Moses asks of us in the Ten Commandments. The Buddhist
prescription for living—the Eightfold Path of Right Understanding,
Right Thought, Right Speech, Right Action, Right Livelihood, Right
Effort, Right Mindfulness, and Right Meditation—is aligned with
what Jesus asks of us in the Beatitudes. What the pinnacle of the
Eastern and Western Religions are asking of us are alike. A certain
obedience.

And just as Jesus turns from the "law of his fathers" to es-
pousing love and forgiveness in the world, the original austere
Theravadin Buddhist traditions are followed by the Mahayana
evolution. The Mahayana emphasis is on the heart and altruism,
the ways of the Bodhisattva, rather than a sole preoccupation with
one's enlightenment. In short, the New Testament becomes to the
Old Testament what Mahayana does for Theravada, an expansion
of the heart. Compassion, not laws and rules, becomes one's spiritual guide.

The Psychology of World Three
The Onset of Anxiety Disorders

The bump in the road is this. In World Three, time, once cyclic
and regenerative, becomes linear and open-ended. History is born.
The individual, once cushioned by group ritual and myth, *becomes*
the myth and in so doing must internalize and enact a portion of
what were once explicit group rituals. Be it seeking Enlightenment
or aligning with the Christ, the individual becomes the primary lo-
cation by which these orientations play themselves out.

As triumphant as these World Religions appear, the psychological consequences of World Three hierarchies are immense. An unprecedented sorrow sweeps the psyche. Depression, wrath, alienation, all kinds of mental and emotional disturbance, begin to plague the species. The first *DSM* psychiatric diagnostic manual could have been written.

As moderns, we still know that territory well. The Gods, the transcendent function, as is their compassionate duty, respond. From the transcendent realms of the Abrahamic faiths (Judaism, Christianity, Islam) to the insightful demands of Jainism, the metaphysical speculations of the Hindu Upanishads, the social critique and "Middle Way" suggestions of the Buddha, the Tao Te Ching wisdom of Lao-tzu (Taoism's mythical master), a global consciousness heaves up in valiant attempts to restore a greater balance.

The question is no longer how do we, as a group, appease and move harmoniously in sync with the forces of nature. It becomes more how do *I*, the emergent individual, rid myself of the burden (and often accompanying shame) of feeling paradoxically both within and torn asunder from society and the natural world. How do we deal with the problems of suffering, alienation, and death? How do we deal with this terrible feeling of aloneness?

For the East, disciplines of yoga and meditation would cultivate silence, the answer beyond words, as the supreme virtue. While the Western faiths also began to offer a monastic, ascetic dimension, the Christian break from cyclic to historical time emphasized a different element. It invented hope. Instead of trying to recover and regenerate a lost Garden of Eden (shamanism), or a liberated self (the East), the advent of history had its Christian followers looking forward to salvation, not at the beginning or outside of, but at the end of time.

While the East and the West have their dramatic differences and effects, a crucial thread connects them. Sacrifice is internalized. The movement to a transcendent Christ parallels the shift from the Vedic world of ritual sacrifice to the Upanishad's *interiorization of sacrifice*, a recognition that it is the lower self, its base desires and attachment to the material world, that must be sacrificed, not an animal or anything outside of one's self:

> Regarding sacrifice as most important, the deluded ones do not know of anything better.... Those who practice austerities and devotion in the forest, the tranquil ones, the knowers of truth, living the life of wandering beggars: they depart, freed from desire, through the door of the sun, to where the immortal Person (Brahman) lives, the imperishable Atman. (*Upanishads* in Fieser 2004)

Like the Upanishads, the Essenes, the ascetic vegetarian religious group who schooled Jesus, went across the grain of its surrounding culture and opposed animal sacrifices. A new kind of inner freedom was sought.

Globally speaking, liberation, salvation, redemption, were at hand. It was to be pursued by a search and release within, not following society's priest-ordered rituals. Fasting, prayer, meditation, and purification were the primary means. This was the transcendental leap of consciousness, the antidote, that World Three offers to its own harsh, caste-driven societies.

On the esoteric side, humanity took a deeper interest in this matter of time. The terrors of historical consciousness had introduced a kind of mortal wounding. In the East, the teachings of karma had replaced the older mythical doctrines of fate with a more accountable and ethic laced metaphysic. The intent was to rid oneself of the shackles of time and body. Similar notions about the reincarnation of the soul would surface in the Greek Mystery Religions and find themselves eloquently expressed in the works of Pythagoras, 500 years before Christ. The soul, in time and space, was not limited to this one body.

But, after the Roman Empire takes over Christianity, what precisely happened to the soul becomes increasingly a legislated political affair. As to be discussed, it would take the esoteric dimensions of World Four to expand for Westerners their understanding of the cycles of life and death. The discipline of psychology would also attempt to come to the rescue for everyone's well being.

The Rise of the World Medical Systems

Just as the world's spiritualities became systemized into the World Religions, so we see the way of ancient shamanic paths organized and codified into world medical systems. While *Apocalyptic* in no way can account for the vast complexity, diversity and evolution by which these new medical systems show up, this much is clear. The planet's first medical systems—the Egyptian (3000 BCE), the Babylonian (2000 BCE), the Ayurvedic (3300 BCE), the Persian (2000 BCE), the Chinese (2700), the Hebrew (2000), the Greek (500 BCE)—all appear as the direct product of World Three empire.

Another layer of the scientific method—the cataloguing and written recording of one's empirical findings—had arrived. Just as the World Religions were addressing the unprecedented alienation of individuals with ethical laced scripture, medical textbooks were addressing the same suffering on the physical plane. The written word—in the hands of shamans turn physicians—becomes a new kind of God.

The essential medical advance is this. In Worlds One and Two, consciousness—as was medical knowledge—was rooted in the interaction of the individual, community and the Universe. While there continue to be great medical truths in recognizing that human health cannot be understood without investigating the *total field* (astral/mental/causal) humans are immersed in, the heightened consciousness of self that the suffering of World Three produces also affords a more precise understanding of the human's overall physiological functioning. The precision with which, for example, Chinese, Ayurvedic, Galenic, and Persian medical systems approached and treated the body, could not have happened in shamanic culture. Consciousness was not yet that inwardly focused.

⬛▶ Culture of the American Southwest:
Old World Hispano

The Spanish, a World Three hierarchal agrarian culture, arrived in Northern New Mexico in the 1540s. They represented the bundle of contradictions that Christianity and European culture had become. They were a culture based on a deep medieval faith, a type of worship in which the saints, as well as Jesus and Mary, much like the Native's kachinas, were considered quite present. They prayed to them daily.

They were also, however, a culture pushed into the vice-grips of the Church and the State, and the fundamentalist efforts to keep the theocratic ordering of their world intact and efficiently imposed on others. Be it populations on the European continent—gypsies, pagan villagers, Jews, women portrayed as demonic witches, the Moors (and in Spain they also went after the Protestants)—or indigenous populations worldwide, the results were bloody. To understand World Three in the American Southwest, we must begin with the Inquisition that forged it.

Over the course of five centuries (1200-1700), much of Europe's rich pagan/Christian cultural mix was whittled down to a barren Protestant ideology and the Catholic Counter-Reformation's attempt to keep pace with the Protestants. Essentially, the Inquisition was about the European tension and conflict between World Two and World Three.

In the horticultural world, the rural village, women had a significant amount of power. In World Three, the Christian and monarchy-driven feudal world wouldn't stand for it. Approximately 80 percent of those killed by the European Inquisition were women—their numbers apparently were in the tens of thousands. The Devil was having, the Church purported, carnal relations with them. The feminine, both within and without, was in deep trouble.

With a return to enforced celibacy for priests in 1073, this was a way in which the Church could also assure none of their property would be handed down to secular offspring. The Inquisition's machinery went into high gear by the mid-1200s. The legal scholars of the Church had sanctioned torture as a way of obtaining confessions, leading to one of the most perplexing periods of human history. The deaths accelerated. In the 16th and 17th centuries, the siege had claimed its greatest toll.

The Renaissance, a rebirth of reason and aesthetic reflection that pronounced the birth of the modern individual, came at nearly the same moment as mass slaughter. On the heels of the Crusades, the Inquisition pogroms were the first massive holocausts that the planet had known. Consequently, the techniques and faith of the old wise women (from whom Paracelsus, the attributed founder of biomedicine's chemical cure, derived much of his knowledge) had been persecuted and legislated out of existence.

And so it is with the contradictions that accompanied the arrival of the Spanish into the American Southwest. The hierarchies of Church and State were feuding. The head clergy excommunicated the governing leaders, and in turn clergy were imprisoned by these leaders. And yet the two hierarchies still managed to form a colonizing pair. From an account of the Spanish Franciscans at the Isleta Pueblo in 1660:

> Fray Salvador de Guerra emerged from his convent one day to find the Indians performing the kachina dance, which he had strictly prohibited. When his repeated exhortations to cease dancing were ignored, the friar stripped himself naked before them, began violently beating himself with a whip, placed a rope around his neck, a crown of thorns on his head, and then crisscrossed the pueblo carrying an enormous cross. When the Indians saw this they immediately stopped their dance, and some, moved to tears by the sight, asked the friar's forgiveness. The others retreated to the safety of their homes, fearing that the Christian soldiers

might soon arrive. (Gutierrez, *When Jesus Came the Corn Mothers Went Away*, 1991)

The Order of St. Francis had turned their patron saint's mission inside out, a kind of self-immolating and overbearing missionary force.

By the 1670s Pueblo spirituals leaders were being burned at the stake. This harsh treatment of the Native eventually led to the Pueblo Revolt of 1680 in which all Franciscans priests were the first to be immediately targeted and killed. The Spanish, after a short period of battle, fled for their lives. The Pueblos might have slaughtered them but, in honor of their own warrior code, simply let them go. Inevitably, the Europeans would be back (1692), their firepower and drive too great. While the Pueblo would attempt to unite for another revolt (1696)—this time unsuccessfully—by 1700 a new type of co-existence emerges. Such are the birth pangs of New Mexico's mestizo population.

Whereas the Inquisition was winding down back in Europe with the birth of the Age of Reason (a topic to be tackled with World Four), the Church and the State were now largely abandoning the New Mexicans in what had become a fierce and fragile frontier. Hunting and gathering tribes (Apache, Ute, Kiowa, Najaho, Comanche), now empowered with the gun and the horse, turned into vengeful raiders on the agrarian peoples. This instigated the Pueblo and the Spanish to align in mutual defense.

With the hierarchies largely gone and forced to fall back on their own instinctual resources, the displaced Spanish settlers returned to their small-scale horticultural village roots. *Penitente* groups, a grassroots religious and brotherhood association, mysteriously appeared throughout the region. Famous for their own flagellation rituals, in fact their primary function was to aid their community.

With the priests largely absent, the Penitentes served whatever religious rituals and civic needs the community had. Church or no Church, the root of this culture exhibited a World Two mystical faith and life of prayer deeply connected to clan and the cycles of nature. Slowly but surely, this affinity of principles with the Native American culture led to all kinds of intermarriage, but not, of course, without some hierarchal resistance.

As conveyed in a 1774 "Description of the Kingdom of New Spain," there were twenty-two different designations of where you fit in on the *casta* list if your blood was less than pure. If a Spanish person married a Native, the child became a *Mestizo*. If a Spanish person married a Mestizo, the child became a *Castizo*. If a Spanish person married a black person, the child became a *Morisco*. If a Spanish person married a Morisco, the child became a *Tornatra*, etc. The only ones not on this caste list were the pure Spanish, but even they were split into a higher and lower class, depending on whether they were born in the New World or the Old World.

This was the European version of the caste system, now transplanted to the indigenous New World. The hierarchy was now based on race. Ironically, at the same time this restrictive caste system was in effect, 70 percent of New Mexico's population was entering into racially mixed marriages. Unlike neighboring Mexico, which still maintains its Spanish elite, by 1800 most of New Mexico's caste system went out the window. Everyone was turning some shade of brown.

New Mexico is the only American state where the minorities have always been the majorities. The full mestizo soul had blossomed (or as a local New Mexican boasts to me, "I am 100-percent mestizo."). This soul was accompanied by the arrival of Our Lady of Guadalupe.

Curanderismo—The Goddess Resurfacing

The Inquisition was well on its way to eliminating Europe's indigenous healers. However, those who made the oceanic passage were able to readily mix their practices in with the accumulated wisdoms of the indigenous Americans. They survived in the New

World, whereas they were snuffed out in the Old. *Curanderismo* is the blended result. In Truchas, New Mexico, an old Spanish mountain village built in the mid-1700s, my neighbor was a *curandera*, a woman who uses massage, a vast knowledge of herbs, and prayer to heal.

A central archetype and motif for her healing, as for the culture at large, is Our Lady of Guadalupe. She is the matriarchal deity figure, whom, in regional Latin Catholicism, Jesus plays second fiddle to. She is the matriarchal figure for the newly forming mestizo. She is the matriarchal deity figure that, as evolution cleverly lurches forward, bridges Worlds.

A few years after the Aztec goddess Tonantzin was suppressed by the Spanish, an apparition of Our Lady appeared to a young Mexican Indian man. The residing Spanish Bishop underwent a radical transformation and decided to build a shrine. This was the New World home for the new mother of a new people, the mestizo, about to be birthed. Our Lady is the mother of the American experiment.

The following is from a Latin American priest based out of San Antonio, Texas. The information in the parenthesis is provided by me:

> The inner recreating power of Guadalupe, its anthropological reversal of the dynamics of conquest, is the declaration that the women will no longer remain silent, passive, and subject to abuse. The introduction of the new paradigm of partnership is the beginning of the end of the patriarchal domination rooted in hierarchal structures imported and imposed by Europe (although the Aztec, Inca and Maya certainly had their own hierarchal injustices as well).... The Nahuatl (Mexico's major Native language and cultural group) philosophers were as fascinated with reality and truth as Aristotle, Plato, and the other great Greek philosophers.
>
> The strength of Nahuatl metaphysics was its emphasis on the interconnectedness and independence of all creation; its limitation or weakness was the submersion of the individual

in the collectivity; even allowing the individual to be sacrificed for the sake of the collectivity. The strength of Western metaphysics has been the isolation and exaltation of the individual; its weakness has been the sacrifice of the collectivity, other individuals, and even the world for the sake of the strongest individual. Both have strengths and disastrous weaknesses. Both need one another to be complete. (Elizondo, *Guadalupe*, 1997)

This is the bridge between the values and beliefs of the tribal Worlds One and Two, and the more stratified World Three and individualized World Four. No matter what side of the bridge we are starting from, we are, today, all mestizos. We are all consciously, and/or unconsciously, attempting to bridge Worlds.

Our Lady of Guadalupe was symptomatic of a larger cultural process, a struggle to restore the feminine/masculine balance that the patriarchies of World Three had disturbed. However strong these patriarchies became, centuries of subterranean cultural streams strived to subvert them *i.e.*, Christianity's early Gnostics, the medieval age of chivalry and the Sufi-influenced troubadours' outpouring of devotional spirit, Hildegard of Bingen boldly suggesting in the 12th century that men and women were equal before God, the 19th century Romantics and Transcendentalists, the modern day feminist and New Age movements.

Perhaps the most powerful surfacing of the ancient goddess archetypes was the widespread medieval devotion to Mary. A celibate priesthood, while of great concern with the empire's institutionalization of Christianity in the fourth century, fell apart in the next one. Up until the twelfth century, certain groups (Cathari, Waldensians) directly appointed women clergy. While Paul of the Bible had seemed to use the Holy Spirit to edit the Holy Mother out of the picture, the common folk would not tolerate it.

Mary appeared in image rather than word, and often in the form of a *black Madonna*. Many medieval churches, extending in a wide arc from Russia across Europe to Spain, had as their most sacred object a statue of a black Mary. (Shlain 1998)

Curiously, it was the Crusades in which Northern Europeans witnessed the Goddess worship of Asia Minor. Statutes of the Black Goddess Isis were creatively revisioned, recreated, and enshrined as the Black Virgin. "Literally hundreds of shrines to the Black Virgin sprang up throughout Europe in the 12th and 13th centuries" (Shlain 1998).

With the notable exception of the Solidarity Movement in Poland, many of these Mary movements have subsided. Noted Jungian analyst Marion Woodman (1996), however, observes that the same archetypal symbols and forces are now pervasively showing up in the modern psyche—our dreams, our longings—in men and women alike. The Goddess will not be kept down. While the Church would not characterize her as such, Our Lady of Guadalupe has become the Western Hemisphere's most renowned Goddess figure.

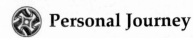 ## Personal Journey

My personal journey with World Three developed as follows. By the ripe age of seventeen years, I sensed that "beneath it all" the world was a very mystical place to be. Little did I know how much that anchor would continue to serve me, in a variety of archetypal forms, throughout my life. Like many in my generation I went screaming away from any type of hierarchal, organized religion and found solace in the Taoist and Native American beliefs and practices that were available to me.

It wasn't until entering into my thirties that I began to long for and crave a deeper, more committed group ritual energy. This first manifested in time spent with Adnan Sarhan, a Sufi master from Baghdad, and shortly thereafter, the Hindu devotional practices associated with Ammachi, one of India's divine mother/guru figures. To enter into both of these two expressions made perfect sense as both elicited and exhibited a *bhakti* devotional heart energy. I wanted to be moved.

I also signed up for ten sessions of Eriksonian hypnotherapy, where the therapist incorporated a past-life component. Whether or not these events actually occurred—that is, were actual past or parallel lives—was secondary, even insignificant, to me. The point is that metaphor and imagery, often from other time and space references, are the ancient ways of the psyche, lending perspective to our current personal dilemmas.

The feeling I've had much of my life upon any time of stress is of literally being speared in the solar plexus. Through hypnotherapy, the story around this was clearly revealed: I was a young, earnest man, a spiritual seeker. I was a Christian, but not of the kind the Roman Empire, which had recently adopted Christianity, would tolerate any longer.

I was, instead, a Christian outside of the hierarchal fold, my knowledge was largely inwardly derived and rigorously earned. I went to the King and begged for mercy, but would not recant my ways. To give that up was to lose everything. To hold on to that was to lose my life. I was, summarily, killed by the King's soldiers who speared me in the solar plexus.

Now whether or not this event ever occurred is, again, incidental. The point is that the psyche, via the techniques of hypnotherapy, provided a kind of metaphoric backdrop for having to operate in a society that largely thought differently than I did. Dreams work in the same manner. This imagery bolstered me.

Next chapter of my life. I took my five precepts as a Buddhist lay practitioner with the anthropologist, mentor, and ordained Zen teacher, Roshi Joan Halifax. This was the first occasion in which, in my potpourri of religious interests, I actually committed to one. Buddha, the *dharma*, and meditation allowed for a kind of personal refuge. This was not as much a religion as a profound exploration, an honoring of a process that could lead to a peace within. Or so I hoped.

A few years later, some ten years after my Christian imagery experience, I was accompanying a group of Thai Buddhist monks on the islands of New Zealand. One of them was an old high school friend who had been a celibate monk for over twenty years. As much as I was trying (or trying not to try) to throw myself over to the Buddha, Christ dreams and imagery kept coming to me. The Buddha path couldn't fully hold me. My internal pathos was too great. Listening to rockin' gospel music in my little monk's retreat, I danced. This was more than just a good beat. An uncanny anointed energy was coming through.

Roshi Joan Halifax with actor Richard Gere

I took my five precepts as a Buddhist lay practitioner with the anthropologist, mentor, and ordained Zen teacher...this was the first occasion in which, in my potpourri of religious interests, I actually committed to one.

Part of this was because I have made a habit of crisscrossing the United States to attend African-American gospel music propelled services. As the 44th President of the United States Barack Obama noted, "Nothing is more powerful than the black church experience. A good choir and a good sermon in the black church, it's pretty hard not to be moved and be transported." (The God Factor: Inside the Spiritual Lives of Public People http://www.amazon.com/God-Factor-Inside-Spiritual-Public/dp/0374530920). What these services, what this music was providing, was a kind of emotional and physical stress release that nothing else seemed to produce. In addition, the more I appealed and prayed to this archetype Christ Jesus, the more it showed up front and center in my psyche.

In returning to the States, I was guided to become a daily devotee of an African-American Christian gospel sound and energy, a healing force through both recordings and live services brought an anointed healing energy to my life and body like no other. My grief needed to bleed out of me.

But it seemed only to happen through joy, not the usual psychological movement to analyze and somehow release the causes of one's situation. The grief seemed to come from some unimaginable deeper level. As the Dalai Lama stated, "If you collected all the tears of sorrow and anguish you have shed in past lives, they would make an ocean larger than any in this universe" (in Fisher, 2002). I gave all my other spiritual pursuits up to became a drummer in praise and worship congregations.

That was nearly a decade ago and I'm still pumping out gospel rhythms. Paradoxically, I was drawn to churches that upheld the very fundamentalism I had been trying to flee. Paradoxically, there was still embedded within the fervency of these expressions, the very anointed energy that I was thirsty for. An oddity in this sea of fundamentalism, I've been both rejected and accepted for this. This is the kind of risk that seems to be asked of us in asserting our own unique archetypal journeys.

Be it from my Christian or Jewish side, the Christ energy came with a terribly tainted amount of baggage. The indigenous foundation was punished, repressed, pushed aside. Eventually, my grandparents on both sides and, more strongly, my parents' generations were all too ready to flee from the carnage. The secularized humanism of World Four, of the modern, provided them immediate refuge. I, however, could only find a partial home there. As the next generation offspring of this secular humanism, I was yearning to know the ways of these older Worlds.

Yogananda

When a liberated Master has dissolved his body in Spirit, and yet manifests in form to receptive devotees (as Jesus has appeared throughout the centuries since his passing...) it means he has an ongoing role to play in the destiny of the world.

But why Jesus? He showed up 500 years after the Buddha. The suffering, especially in his part of the hierarchal world, had dramatically increased. Detachment was a much more difficult, perhaps impossible task. As portrayed in the vast iconography of these two celestial masters, whereas the Buddha skillfully separates himself from the pain, Jesus visibly exhibits the suffering for all of the world to see.

Paramahansa Yogananda (*Autobiography of a Yogi*) was a teacher, who through his presence, writings, and founding of the Self-Realization Fellowship, helped introduce Eastern Religions to the West. Little did people know that in his lifetime, he was a great follower of Christ. In the posthumously published two volume set, *The Second Coming of Christ—The Resurrection of the Christ Within You*, Yogananda skillfully explained the archetypal phenomena that was happening to me:

> It is an erroneous assumption of limited minds that great ones such as Jesus, and their divine incarnations are gone from the earth when they are no longer visible to human sight. This is not so. When a liberated Master has dissolved his body in Spirit, and yet manifests in form to receptive devotees (as Jesus has appeared throughout the centuries since his passing...) it means he has an ongoing role to play in the destiny of the world. (Yogananda 2004)

Be it the Buddha or the Christ, or some other integration of the World Religions, *the tensions that the evolution into hierarchal societies created also invited the disciplines and contemplative consciousness to manage and transcend such tensions.*

El Padre Salsa

Curiously, one of the most popular priests in today's New Mexico is Father Frank Pretto, also known as *El Padre Salsa*. Actually born into a Jewish family in Panama, he converted in high school—on, of all days, Yom Kippur—to Catholicism. It took him a whole year to muster the courage to tell his parents. Meanwhile, while learning scales on the piano as "young Frankie," he couldn't help but notice the hot sounds (meringue, cumbia, mambo) in the Panama streets (just as in my brief classical piano tradition, all I wanted to do was play boogie-woogie.)

Pretto ended up going to university, as he said, in a "strange town called Albuquerque." The brother of one of the people in his high school salsa combo was attending University of New Mexico. A semester away from graduating with a degree in business administration and accounting, Pretto dropped out. He realized he was really supposed to be a priest and joined the seminary. Bombshell number two.

The reason why I share all of this is Father Pretto bridges the more sense oriented catharsis of Worlds One and Two ritual (that the Catholic Church had largely divorced itself from) with the Christ he so profoundly felt, worshipped, and preaches about. In short, Pretto restores and marries passion with faith. The Archbishop wisely allowed Pretto to play salsa in the nightclubs on Friday nights, and attend to his flock the rest of the week. Pretto became so popular a much bigger parish church was built for him, the opposite of the downsizing this faith is experiencing elsewhere.

Tactfully bridging the gap between institutionalized religion and nightclub entertainment, Pretto addresses and heals a schism that lies at the heart of the Western spiritual world. In a personal interview, Pretto explained:

> As a priest and musician, if I didn't have one or the other there would be something lacking. I really don't believe that religion can fulfill as such. There's a very big difference between religion and spirituality. A person can have a tremendous spiri-

tuality without being religious, or a person could be religious without even knowing God at all, as is the case with so many people. I experience music as the ultimate high. It is not only an avenue to the Almighty but also a tremendous vehicle to people. I feel one with people in all of these things I do.

In short, this priest rocks.

I aim for the same bridge with the addicts I work by facilitating drum circles. I allow and encourage a deeply passionate energy to come out. This needs to be expressed. It is in this honoring of and restoring deep expressive channels that the twisted, hierarchal energies of World Three begin to find a redemptive, transcendent sphere. There is no way around this energy, just skillfully through it.

⬛ Practical Applications

Heroin is the God drug. You want instant delivery, there it is. Generally associated with the inner city, heroin has pervaded all kinds of demographic terrain. Suburban white, upper middle class chic, the ultimate party high. In the county I live and work in, sandwiched in between the gentrification of the Taos and Santa Fe communities and counties, the highest drug overdose rate per capita in the country has persisted for the last decade. The predominant cause is heroin. God is sorely needed.

Why would this be in a county that is 90 percent Native American and Hispanic, where community-oriented spiritual traditions still run deep. The heroin phenomenon here is nearly entirely among the Spanish, or what in this chapter has been explored as a "mestizo" culture and consciousness. The trauma started as a clash between Worlds. Just as the Spanish conquered the Native tribes, a little more than a century ago, the American government and frontier peoples pulled the lands out from under this mestizo culture.

New Mexico's Spanish farming communities had adhered to a communal principle of property ownership, Europe's medieval land grant system. Where families maintain their own private homes, gardens and lots, most of the land was held in common for hunting, farming, grazing and timber purposes. These communal land grants had no place in the aggressive push of capitalist incentive and private property. The individualistic, entrepreneurial drive of World Four did not know how to honor this older, communal manner of adjudicating land. By the early 1900s an estimated 80 percent of the Spanish land grants ended up in the hands of Anglo-American lawyers and settlers. Like some Native American communities, most of the Spanish lands were seized through the trickery of the American legal system.

The clash was cultural as well. The American land grab was married with the philosophy of Manifest Destiny, the Protestant-fueled ideology that it was the American inevitability to colonize and Christianize all other peoples in its path. The medieval Catholicism of the Spanish, the Protestantism the new Americans brought, were too very different expressions. The one was about cultivating a rich inner dialogue with divinity bolstered by community worship and support, the other a fairly barren inner world driven by an entrepreneurial individualism that would be rewarded by riches and/or a better afterlife. The two were in for a mighty collision.

The trauma that hit indigenous cultures at this country's inception some 500 years ago, was now hitting these agrarian, mestizo cultures little more than a century ago. When agrarian cultures lose their land they lose their community base, which is connected to their own sense of self-worth. A few generations later there is then amnesia about the origins of that trauma. But, the experience of trauma remains. It's all around. This is the trauma—several generations later—that is still showing up in my psychotherapist office.

As a counselor and teacher I have been working with this population for the last twenty years. I have worked with heroin addicts and gangsters. I have worked with their families. I've had a few clients murdered. I've had a few clients sentenced for murder. *Machismo*, the Spanish code of honor that asks us to serve and protect our family and community, gets twisted into an ugly, masculine urge to bully and dominate. The masculine, stripped of its resource and pride, goes desperately out of balance.

In my work with heroin addicts, this is where I start: how to rebalance cultural values that don't seem to fit into a modern world. If a culture's land and modus operandi have been stripped away, its spiritual archetypes can't hold the same sway. They even seem like a source of failure and shame. The aim is to restore that integrity, to trust that in piecing together a shattered psyche and cultural world-view, a more viable and lasting bridge can be built with the modern world.

Much, rightfully so, has been made of the cultural genocide that landed upon the indigenous, tribal peoples of this planet. But there are also 5,000 years of theocratically-ordered cultures, Islam being the most pronounced, that are struggling equally with how and if to modernize. This explains the "machismo" tension besetting these cultures, a quest to hold on to an ancient code of honor that can result in patriarchal and terrorist extremes. My work as a cultural psychologist is to honor the code, not dismiss it or try to readily transform it into a value system more palatable to my modern sense of gender equality

There is no culture in today's world that has not been touched by hierarchy. There is no one that has not been affected (and infected) by World Three. The temptation is to make a simplified division from this: indigenous *good*, hierarchy *bad*. Evolution and our psyches are much too complex to take this way out. Hierarchy, after all, is laced into nature. Animals naturally dominate one another and it is a rather bold experiment for humans to think they can do otherwise.

The quest here is to find in what ways oppression and internalized oppression in your own heritage and upbringing have played a role in your own personal evolution. This is not about holding on to a blame and victim mentality, or inversely, one of shame and guilt. This is, rather, a coming out of denial, an understanding that the pitfalls of human history parallels, indeed, fills in our own personal story.

In conscious recognition of how the energies of this history have played themselves out in our societies and families, we are then able to see the same process within ourselves. Therapeutic applications include, foremost, coming fully into touch with how well one is managing one's own personal power, and in what ways the powers of others and society may have a hold over you. From another angle: In what ways are you, and do you allow yourself to be, disempowered?

As the World Religions have heavily impacted so many of us, this is also an opportunity to explore in what ways those archetypes have been at play in your life. What in your belief system needs to be sorted through and discarded, and what possible techniques (meditation, prayer) might be called on?

There are very few on the planet who have not been touched somehow by one of the World Religions: the Abrahamic faiths, the Eastern expressions of Taoism, Hinduism, Buddhism and Sikhism. With whatever damage the theocratic applications of those religions may have incurred, there is, assuredly, a divine light at the end of any one of those tunnels. A courageous adventure might need to be undertaken to "wrestle" a religion away from its institutionalized expression and back into the domain of personal revelation and faith. Depending on one's societal setting, how one conducts this journey must be cleverly done. Theocracies, generally speaking, don't like to be questioned.

At different times in my life, and in this order, this has meant engaging the archetypes that have enticed and resonated within me: Hinduism's bhakti, Islam's passionate Sufi practices, the Buddha's contemplative compassion, the prayerful mercy of Christ. In this way I embody an antidote to hierarchy's abuses.

When and how this same unfolding occurs in the people I am working with has its own very delicate timing, its own grace. I am there to provide an unconditional anchor for the tensions of World Three as I work that tension out within myself.

*Clearly there is too much historical complexity to adequately cover the intricate terrain of World Three. But fortuitously, the way this complexity unfolds aligns itself with the body/heart/mind/spirit poles of the ancient Medicine Wheel. The principles of the Medicine Wheel, while tribal in origin, can be seen equally in cultures dominated by hierarchy and empire. Though more complex, as history and culture have become more complex, the quest for integration—the body/heart/mind/spirit link—remains constant.

World Three Medicine Wheel (Western)

Clearly there is too much historical complexity to adequately cover the intricate terrain of World Three. But fortuitously, the way this complexity unfolds aligns itself with the body/heart/mind/spirit poles of the ancient Medicine Wheel. The principles of the Medicine Wheel, while tribal in origin, can be seen equally in cultures dominated by hierarchy and empire. Though more complex, as history and culture have become more complex, the quest for integration—the body/heart/mind/spirit link—remains constant.

The Greek/Christian Medicine Wheel

In explaining the Medicine Wheel of Western culture and the uncanny sway the Christ would have on people's psyche, we must begin with the earlier Greek version of it. The Greeks, like their East Indian counterparts, were the philosophical geniuses of the Western World.

South – the Body

In the South, the body, a peculiar dualism pervades Greek culture. The Spirit is trapped in the body and must be freed. The Greek Olympian ideal of the body, the perfection of the body's mass and movement, would counteract that to some extent. The body gets to be fully embodied.

West – the Heart

It was this predominant pull to be released from the body that sends Greek culture hurtling into the emotional dynamics of the West, resulting in the cathartic rituals of the mystery religions. At the pinnacle of this expression, Dionysus transforms the hedonistic risks of the physical senses into transcendent engagement (akin to tantra in the East). Emotions were entered to purge themselves. This is the ritual matrix (talking in talks, slain in the Spirit) that the later followers of Jesus would spring off of to come to know the Christ. This is the *bhakti*, the devotional depths of the West.

North – the Mind

The cognitive pole of the North introduced a Greek rationalist mindset that presented a fully secularized modern point of view centuries before its time. Some twenty-five hundred years ago, "from Thales and Anaximander to Leucippus and Democritus, a naturalistic science matured in step with an increasingly skeptical rationalism...Man and society were to be studied, methodically and empirically, without theological preconceptions. Myths were to be understood as allegorical fables, not revelations of a divine reality." (Tarnas, *The Passion of the Western Mind*, 1993)

East – the Spirit

The passionate, theatrical nature of the Greek soul, however, could not comfortably sit with this bland agnosticism. The Eastern pole of this Greek Medicine Wheel, Plato's "ideal form," synthesizes the tension the West and North present. There is a divine order beneath the *cacophony* of the sense-based world, and it is via a radical turning inwards that one comes to know this. This is the *Logos*, the archetype in its purest form. It was one small step from the Logos, the pattern of the Universe, to the Christ, this same divine order that also dwells within.

In their understanding of Christ as the incarnate Logos, early Christians synthesized the Greek philosophical doctrine of the intelligible divine rationality of the world with the Judaic religion doctrine of the creative Word of God. (Tarnas 1993).

God, no longer some distant entity governed by fate, shows up in the innermost pattern of the human soul. Sufficiently cleanse the doors of perception and the two, God and human, become One.

Eastern Medicine Wheel
For all their apparent differences, the Eastern Medicine Wheel doesn't proceed all that differently. This commonality indicates the universality that the World Religions uphold.

South – the Body
The South pole of the Wheel, the body, shows up in the ancient science of yoga. This, too, was dualistic in origin. *Yoga*, to yoke, to unite, was the attempt of freedom from the constraints of the body. Tantra, its opposite but complementary partner, was the journey to embrace the body/senses based world, but from a detached exalted realm.

West – the Heart
This is known as *bhakti*, the outpouring of the devotional heart. Shiva is Dionysus' thematic cousin. Most Hindu ritual is bhakti in nature.

North – the Mind
The sophisticated analytical worldview that Buddhism presents fills out the cognitive North pole of the Medicine Wheel. The philosopher Nagarjuna (3rd century BCE), through the notion of dependent co-origination, laid out a profound understanding of how thought and the Universe alike are structured. Nothing exists in and of itself. Everything is in relationship. This forecasts some 2000 years ago the principles of Einstein's theory of relativity.

East – The Spirit
The pole of the East posits a kind of archetypal arrival—*moksha, Samadhi, nirvana, satori*—that goes beyond archetype. While not personally incarnated through Jesus the Christ, there are enlightened masters that indicate this evolutionary leap in consciousness.

World Three Summary

With the advent of empire, there was a shift into patriarchal, hierarchal societies. Levels and abuses of power were introduced on to the planet that we, as a species, have still not fully healed and struck a balance with. The tribal world had gone amuck, much of this fueled by expanding demographics of populations that led inevitably to kill and conquer scenarios.

At first these new hierarchies tried to ensure order by the "divine right" of kings. Oppression and injustice, however, continued to increase. Religious expressions emerged that attempted to find refuge and forgiveness for the alienation the average citizen was now experiencing. Eventually pulled into the very hierarchies they were critiquing, these expressions came to be known as the World Religions.

Global Archetypal Unfolding
History Arrives as His Story
The advent of hierarchal societies occurs on all continents with the exception of Australia. This coincides with the rise of writing, law and conquering warfare.

Divine Kingship
Government shifted from egalitarian oriented tribal organization to pyramidal hierarchies. Leaders were supposed to represent a divine will speaking through them, but were also prone, as was hierarchy, to corruption and indulgence.

The Hero in a New World
The lack of tribal cohesion and support leads to the emergence of the "alone" individual. This leads to an *ego consciousness* seeking to resolve its own inbuilt anguish.

Birth of the World Religions

The *axial period of history* creates "ethical imperatives" and "meditational/prayer regimes" demanding individuals hold up standards of conduct that caste-structured societies no longer could. This sets the foundations for the World Religions—the Abrahamic Faiths in the West, the Hindu/Buddhist lineages in the East—that were respectively interested in the salvation and liberation of the human soul.

Loss of the Feminine

An estimated ninety percent of female deities, and along with their feminine principles, are lost or submerged culturally underground with these new patriarchal driven World Religions.

The Abrahamic Faiths

While seemingly the creation of a small tribe known as the Hebrews, these faiths integrate the diverse influences of the entire Middle East and Mediterranean cultures. With the 4th century Roman institutionalization of Christianity, the vast array of Gnostic Christian expressions are eliminated or forced underground. Islam is born two centuries later trying to create the theocratic nation the Jews were unable to.

The Journey of the East

The ancient wisdom traditions of Jainism and Hinduism find a synthesis in the "investigative psychology" that Buddhism proposes. Altogether they form the core to Eastern Religions, although the East is much more tolerant of the older shamanic and newer contemplative layers of culture melding together. Much like the West, empire is the order of the day, while these advances in consciousness offer a kind of personal reprieve.

Where East Meets West

For all of their purported differences, the World Religions provide new personal disciplines and ethical standards to help sustain societies that have become all too harshly driven by hierarchy.

The Psychology of World Three

An unprecedented kind of alienation hits the species, a combination of people falling through society's cracks with no safety net and a terrifying open-ended concept of time and history that the circular/seasonal nature of tribal life was protected from. Mental illnesses become epidemic.

The Rise of the World Medical Systems

Because of a more focused awareness and attention on the "alienated Self," combined with hierarchal structures that pervade all dimensions of culture, medicine becomes systematized. From Chinese and Ayurvedic in the East to Galenic and Arabic advances in the West, the more amorphous calling of the shaman funnels into rigorously trained healers the modern knows as doctors.

🜚 Culture of the American Southwest

Old World Hispano

The culture the Spanish brings to the New World contains a bundle of contradictions. While the Inquisition cracks down on the indigenous peoples, many of the transplanted southern Europeans, akin to the Natives, live a small-scale village life with a deep agrarian-based faith. Once the Inquisition is dismantled, mestizo culture begins to blossom.

Curanderismo - The Goddess Resurfacing

A tradition that did not survive the witch-craze of the 16th and 17th centuries, the New World *curandera* represents a blend of the European healers with Amerindian knowledge of herbs and healing. Our Lady of Guadalupe becomes a symbol of this integration, indicating both the ancient love for Mary, the Mother of God, and the importance the Goddess played in Native American culture.

Personal Journey

My own spiritual journey ranges from hypnotherapy to devotional practices from the World Religions.

Practical Applications

My work as a counselor with addiction, dysfunction, and trauma that are clearly a result of the clash and tension between the indigenous and hierarchal Worlds.

THE MODERN WORLD VIEW

WORLD FOUR
Industrialization:
The Mechanistic Paradigm

COGNITIVE

PSYCHO-
DYNAMICS

ARCHETYPAL/
HUMANISTIC

BEHAVIORISM

First Onset:

1600s

Predominant Infrastructure:

INDUSTRIAL

Predominant Social Structure:

NUCLEAR / BROKEN FAMILY, SOCIAL MOBILITY

Predominant Superstructure:

SECULARIZATION, FREE WILL

Predominant Medicinal Response:

BIOMEDICINE

Predominant Mode of Thinking:

MENTAL, ANALYTICAL

Human Potential Advance:

INDIVIDUATION

Shadow Sides:

CAPITALIST / CULTURAL IMPERIALISM, SELFISHNESS

American Southwest Culture:

AMERICAN ARRIVAL

Personal Journey:

RECONNECTING WITH MY PERSONAL ANCESTORS

Global Archetypal Unfolding
Liberation and Death

There's much about the arrival of World Four that carries over from World Three. Hierarchy and injustice still prevail. The collusion of religion and government are the predominant ordering of the times. The doctrines of liberation and salvation have been fully mainstreamed, but soon will be equally sought in all kinds of private spheres apart from this societal grip. A momentous groundswell, a scientific followed by an industrial revolution, will slowly but surely rip this societal ordering to pieces.

This new World is one that will largely start and evolve with only the European peoples. But it is only a matter of a few centuries before the whole planet is affected. The Reformation and Counter-reformation, industrialization, the breaking up of Church and State, the rise of capitalism and democracy, were about to change the global landscape.

Imperialism would never go away. The mass migration of European peoples and African slaves to the Americas, as well as the colonization of all the other continents, would guarantee that. It was, however, as we see throughout the *Apocalyptic Grace*, an internal transformation that would more pointedly define modern consciousness. The Age of Reason followed by Industrialization, leads to a kind of diminishing of the fuller territories of the soul. Soul, however, as is the soul's nature, won't stand for it.

As this chapter will unfold in bold generalized strokes, the formation of the modern world may not seem all that pleasant. A lot of cultures and the ways of the ancients are threatened or lost. We become strangely secularized creatures. And, as the wars and holocausts of the last century demonstrate, we are no less prone to violence. But the more pronounced violence was occurring within.

Consciousness had turned "flat," or as German philosopher Nietzsche forewarned the 20th century, our Gods no longer exist because we have killed them. However, a great liberation—for women, children, slaves, and societal inequalities based on race, ethnicity, and creed—was also in the making. Whatever the downsides, evolution, as always, has its purpose and crowning moments. The new incongruities are, however, rather startling. Humanity sees its greatest movements of liberation and violent death happening at the same time.

The esoteric streams of the entire Renaissance that the Inquisition forced underground would not stay submerged for long. As has been a persistent theme, anything pushed down in culture smolders for a while and then often roars back with whole new combinations of possibilities. The unprecedented rise of the arts, entertainment, and sports surfaced as 20th century secularized religions.

In addition, by the end of the century a revived interest in shamanism and the esoteric dimensions of the world religions, generically referred to as the New Age, had infiltrated mainstream consciousness. And finally, psychology, that territory by which we give ourselves permission to explore ourselves, becomes the talk of the town. Altogether, these movements compensated for the "flatlands" that modern consciousness had induced. Alas, all kinds of addiction, most notably drugs and alcohol, would also try to fill the same void.

Downsizing the Imagination

Again, the cultural territory that creates World Four is too vast and complex to do it justice in one chapter. My intention here is to track the prominent tensions occurring on the European continent that forged the modern point of view and way of life. We must first return to that dreaded Inquisition, and actually it's dismantling, as a way of understanding how this piece of history created the foundation for the scientific and industrial revolutions.

The transformations that created this shift in consciousness were a sequence of dialectical tensions that first separated the Middle Ages from the Renaissance, and then spilled into an entirely novel definition of social order and personal psychology. This is truly a period of Enlightenment, but its emphasis on the empirical and rational realms were often the opposite of how Eastern Religions would come to use this term.

While the Church can be seen as a corrupted hierarchy, the opposite truths hold as well. The Church held the ground for the most advanced intellectual activity of the European continent. Much of the scientific and metaphysical wisdom of antiquity, particularly Greek and Egyptian knowledge, finds fertile grounds in the scholastic awakening of the 12th and 13th centuries.

Thomas Aquinas (1225-1274), in the spirit of the Church's thematic founder, Augustine, and his guide, Aristotle, entertains a deep marriage of *Reason* and *Faith*. The manner in which the mind acquires knowledge illuminates the truths of nature. Ironically, it is the Arabic maintaining and advancing upon these ancient wisdom traditions that kept the fires of science and medicine alive for a European continent still crawling out of the Dark Ages. Without this Islamic link, there would have been no Renaissance.

The Dominicans, and later the Jesuits, continue this monastic scholarly tradition. This will culminate in the 14th century with Francecso Petrarch (1304-1374), considered the granddaddy of modern day humanism. The discovery of the letters of Cicero, an ancient orator of classical Greek humanism, and then the dissemination of these ideas by Erasmus (1466-1536), gave Humanism its central drive. The seeds of the moderns' penchant for a well rounded education are sown.

Two trends, one more heart oriented, the other distinctly rationally minded, accompany this humanistic bent. On the one hand, there are those thirsty for reinvesting religious archetypes with devotional mysticism, a kind of *bhakti* of the West. Perhaps most revolutionary was Hildegard of Bingen (1098-1178), a woman centuries before her time. Among a vast array of talents, Hildegard was known as a theologian, composer, and natural healer. She boldly proposed that women and men are equal in the eyes of the Lord, and, in a scientifically veiled manner, wrote about the experience of the female orgasm. A sufferer of chronic migraine headaches, Hildegard attributed her abilities to know God as a result of the quest to find peace with her condition.

On her heels, the "back to the essence of Christianity" (and nature) movement launched by St. Francis (1182-1226) become so popular the Church has no choice but to bring these devotees back into the fold. The religious rebel ends up managing a Church sanctioned ecclesiastic order, the Franciscans. Not very good at management, Francis bows out of his own Order in his lifetime.

On a more esoteric plane, Meister Eckhart (1260-1328) spearheads a contemplative approach to God that parallels Buddhism's ventures into *nothingness*. Advocating prayer, rather than priest-governed ritual, as the strongest, most immediate way to know God, the Church cannot help but feel threatened. A couple of centuries later, St. John of the Cross (1542-1591) and his mentor, Teresa of Avila (1515-1582), would experience similar "existential journeys" and go through similar societal trials. Characterized by St. John as "the dark night of the soul," it is, again, through the shadow side of our being—our doubts, our anguish—in which we come to know God so much deeper.

Meanwhile, on the level of everyday culture, courtly love, via the entertaining troubadours, spurs on a whole new religion of the heart. For eons considered the offshoot of the economic arrangement of marriage, romance becomes a pedestal unto itself. Curiously again, Islam plays a central role here. The troubadours had a direct Sufi devotional influence. The love we feel for our beloved is on par with the love we feel for our God (and vise-versa). In Christian terms, the love we feel for Mary, the deep feminine Mother of God, is interchangeable with the love that shows up in our eroticized relationships.

The other opposing trend is an increasing *agnosticism*. Averroes, an Arabic philosopher-scientist (1126-1198), is reintroduced as the pillar by which one can best come to know the natural elements of the world. This trend culminates in the figure of a relatively obscure scholar, William of Ockham (1288-1348), who takes Greek rationalism to its logical extreme. While God is most certainly real, we can't really know him. At best, we can accurately name the contents of our Reality. This *Nominalism* would by the 1700s become the order of the day. The mechanistic philosophy would beckon to become World Four's front-and-center paradigm. The European continent was in for a mighty collision.

Neoplatonism

New arrivals and translations of ancient Greek works in the 15th century provided fresh inspiration. Neoplatonism, an evolutionary branch of Humanism and the direct foundation of modern science, continues the humanist exploration in a fresh direction. The Hermetic and alchemist traditions are subcultures within this broad Neoplatonic movement. The prominent Neoplatonists—Copernicus, Paracelsus, Kepler, Fludd, Bruno, Ficino, Dee, and indeed Sir Isaac Newton himself—are considered to be the first legitimate modern scientists. They were more accurately the last of the *magi*, a group of proto-scientists deriving their knowledge from an ancient way of looking at things.

Their quest was to match the majesty of God's creations with empirical, mathematical proof. They married an ancient scientific awareness, derived largely from Egyptian, Persian and Greek knowledge, with experimental zeal. In effect, they synthesized the best of ancient rationalist endeavor with piety and a profound sense of how God went about creating *order* in all things. Perhaps the most stunning synthesis came from the astronomer Johannes Kepler (1571-1630). Kepler understood gravity and the planets as "the music of the spheres," and saw his profession as "priests of the most high God with respect to the book of nature" (Tarnas 1993).

That these endeavors were about magic obscures, from the modern perspective, what their true nature was. This was "magic" not of a demonic nature as attributed to it by the persecutors of

the witch-craze, nor of the mystical sentimentalism generally as-
cribed to it by the modern's scientific paradigm. Instead, we see a
profound ancient cosmology that links the depths of religion and
scientific inquiry:

> Magick is nothing else but the survey of the whole course
> of nature. For whilst we consider the Heavens, the Stars, the
> Elements, how they are moved, and how they are changed,
> by this means we find out the hidden secrecies of living crea-
> tures, of plants, of metals, and of their generation and corrup-
> tion; so that this whole science seems merely to depend upon
> the view of Nature. (Porta 1558 in Debus 1977)

This kind of thinking was revived in the Renaissance, most notably
with Marsilio Ficino's translation (1463) of the *Corpus Hermeticum*.
Named after the mythical figure Hermes Trismegestus (meaning
thrice-great), and identified by the Greeks with the Egyptian God
Thoth (as mentioned in the chapter on World Three), the Hermetic
tracts are now believed to have been organized by an anonymous
group of Greeks at the beginning of the Christian era. They contained a Greek philosophical mixture of Platonism and Stoicism,
along with Jewish and Persian Gnostic influences.

Gnosticism, persecuted by the Roman's 4th century appropriation of Christianity, and seemingly extinct, again rears its head.
The Renaissance translation of ancient texts pouring back into Europe would assure that. Texts that made it into the Bible had other
renditions and interpretations. *Pimander*, the opening tract of the
Corpus Hermeticum, and the Book of Genesis, are amazingly nearly identical, with one vital difference. Whereas in Genesis a fall is
recorded, in Pimander God grants humans the ability to recapture
the state from which they have fallen through the divine powers
God has granted them:

> All the power of magic consists in love. The work of magic
> is the attraction of one thing by another in virtue of their nat-
> ural sympathy. The parts of the world, like the members of
> one animal are united among themselves in the community
> of a single nature. From their communal relationship a com-

mon love is born and from this love a common attraction: and this is the true magic...thus, the lodestone attracts iron, amber straw, brimstone fire, the Sun draws flowers and leaves toward itself, the Moon the Seas. (Ficino 1463 in Easlea 1980)

Love is the glue to the Universe. An ancient animism is about to spur on the birthing of a new science.

It is not coincidental that this combination of resurrected Hermetic doctrine, the northerly spread of the Kabbalah traditions revived in medieval Spain, and Neoplatonism (largely drawn from 3rd century Greek philosopher Plotinus), would unite in the Renaissance. All three last met in the Christian influenced Gnosticism of the early centuries CE. These same principles that informed pre-Christian Greek and Middle Eastern culture, and carried over into pre-Roman Christianity, were now resurfacing to fuel the scientific revolution. The center, however, will not hold. The last of European tribal culture was on its way out. The Neoplatonists were pulled into the fray.

Crazed about Witches

As we have reviewed, the Renaissance, while generally attributed to be the genesis of modern day humanism and reason, was actually, through these Neoplatonic movements, as much interested in uncovering and advancing a mystically based Science of the Universe. While as a whole Humanism lends itself to secularization and the triumph of the individual, the broader scope of Neoplatonism trusts that the magnificence of God possesses a sacred order that can be mathematically explained (or, in the 20th century words of Albert Einstein, "God doesn't play dice with the Universe"). What these two traditions had in common was the attempt to revitalize a continent worn out by the hierarchy of Christianity. The Reformation (1517) would beat them to the punch.

The Reformation is, rightly so, seen as the needed libertarian critique of an indulgent Catholic institution. However, it ironically also creates a Biblical backlash, one akin to the modern Christian fundamentalism that pervades today's conservative congregations. Common people were beginning to read and more easily get their hands on the Bible produced by the recently invented printing press.

The Catholic hierarchy is effectively undermined. People no longer need the priest to mediate God for them. The religious pluralism that is being caused by the movements of Humanism and Neoplatonism are equally suspect. Their incorporation of ancient, broader educational, philosophical and spiritual possibilities—although still considerably Christ centered—feels like disguised pagan worship.

The Catholic Church has no choice but to respond. They begin through the Council of Trent (1545-1563), otherwise known as the Counter-Reformation, to clean up their act. Alongside the heirs of the Reformation, they go after a common enemy: all of those falling outside of or stretching the boundaries of a strict Bible based cosmology. Starting in the 12th century, the Inquisition hit high gear in the Renaissance. It was this witch-craze phenomena, a period of persecution and prosecution that peaked in the 16th century and began to dwindle by the mid-17th, that brought a crushing blow to this revitalization of Ancient Middle Eastern lineages.

The witch-craze went after two elements: Neoplatonism and the rural, predominantly women, healers. The new scientists, while some were employed within the Church, were now considered a threat:

> The scientific revolution of the sixteenth and seventeenth centuries, it is now generally agreed owed more to the new Platonism of the Renaissance, and to the Hermetic mysticism which grew out of it, than to any mere "rationalism" in the modern sense of the word. Ficino with his "natural magic", Paracelsus for all of his bombast, Giodordano Bruno in spite of his "Egyptian" fantasies, did more to advanced the concept and investigation of a regular "Nature" than many a rational

sensible Aristotelian scholar who laughed at their absurdities or shrank from their shocking conclusions...It is no accident that "natural magicians" like Agrippa, and "alchemists" like Paracelsus and his disciples were among the enemies of the witch-craze, while those who attacked Platonist philosophy, Hermetic ideas and Paracelsian medicine were also, often, the most stalwart defenders of the witch craze. (Trevor-Roper, *The European Witch-craze of the 16th and 17th Centuries*, 1969)

Similarly, the rural wise woman, maintaining a kind of tribal power in her village, was a direct affront to the urbanized Christianity trying now to colonize the entire European continent.

When the dust settled, Ockham's nominalism—*what you see is what you get*—forms a strange marriage with this Inquisitional dominance. The most advanced achievements of Europe's World Three, the powerful discoveries of the founders of modern medicine and science, were to be recast into a whole new paradigm. World Four was born.

In the 1540s we are in the world of Copernicus and Paracelsus; the one a hesitant, tradition bound, secretive ecclesiastic whose "revolutionary" Heliocentric theory was little more than a re-discovery of the ancients; the other a fantastical medical practitioner with unorthodox cures and a profound belief in "natural philosophy" and magic. By 1660, with the foundation of the Royal Society of London, we are in the empirical, experimental world of Boyle and Newton, a world in which God was an external maintenance rather than an immanent spirit. (Kaamen in Hirst and Wooley, *Social Relations and Human Attributes*, 1982)

What must be stressed here is that the machinery that created the witch-craze and defeated a revived Gnosticism had also spawned the scientific Enlightenment. And yet, while substantially built, the machinery had still not largely produced its products, that is, the industrial revolution of the 18th century. Instead, it had already guaranteed its own inbuilt survival; the means to eliminate certain kinds of indigenous European beliefs, alongside parallel Gnostic intellectual traditions, linked to earlier Worlds.

The witch-craze and the Reformation had this combined effect on the ancient ways of the peoples of Europe. By the mid-1600s, incantations, dancing, maypoles, bagpipes and fiddle music, seances, gift exchanges were either entirely banned or considerably curtailed across the British Isles and the European continent. Shrines were dismantled and hymns revoked within the fear they had been conceived as magic spells. The conjuring of spirits and the practicing of alchemy were deemed acts of felony.

Whereas the history of such persecutions reflected the intellectual assumptions of the upper, educated classes controlling the courts, witch accusations must also be understood within the context of the immediate environment, the village life, where they also occurred. Charms and spiritual defenses were the standard villagers means for combating illness, stress and misfortune. Ironically, it was actually the very infiltration of Protestant ideologies that kept the power of the witches alive for a while longer. People needed some explanation for the calamity of their lives. God's Will was no longer easily accessible. The most that one could hope for was that those who endured the hardships of this world would be rewarded in the afterlife. The villagers, thus, often had each other to look to and to blame when life's difficulties became overwhelming.

The paradox is that many would just as quickly turn to some of these same outlawed people for immediate relief. As renowned statesmen and philosophers Thomas Hobbes and Francis Bacon respectively conceded, "I would rather have the advice or take physic from an experienced old woman that had been at many sick people's bedside, than from the learned but inexperienced physician," that "empirics and old women were more happy many times in their cure than learned physicians" (in Debus, *The Chemical Philosophy: Paracelsian Medicine in the 16th and 17th centuries*, 1977).

This, however, also was about to shift.

The Mechanical Philosophy

A new paradigm, the mechanistic philosophy, was entering; it would take the fruits of the Neoplatonists' empirical method but strip it of its metaphysical foundation. At the forefront were the French mechanists Mersenne and Gassendi. In response to "an ever increasing interest in Rosicrucian and alchemical mysticism," Mersenne recommended that academics "police the field, not only by punishing charlatans, but also by actively engaging in the reforms of science" (Easlea 1980).

Terms and disciplines such as *Christiano-cabalistique, Divino magique, Physio-chemique,* and the like would be discarded, while in their place would be substituted a clear terminology based upon chemical operations performed in the laboratory. A reformed alchemy would steer clear of religious, philosophical and theological questions, which were of absolutely no concern" (Easlea 1980). Gassendi's "corpuscular mechanical philosophy" offers a re-appropriation of ancient Greek atomistic thought in which "reality comprised only the moving atoms and the void, with no other existent, no spiritual or immaterial entity" (Easlea 1980).

The declaration of their colleague Rene Descartes, *"I think, therefore I am,"* forms the basis of the Cartesian philosophy that would underlie this new scientific worldview. As Descartes asserted, there are "no qualities so occult nor effects of sympathy or antipathy so marvelous or strange" that their properties cannot be explained in terms of the "size, shape, situation, and motion of different particles of matter" (Easlea 1980).

These are the effects. The mechanistic world could no longer be rendered redeemable in transcendental refuge. The paradox of a now hidden God, omnisciently present but forever mute, coincides with the emergence of us moderns. Community is no longer God centered. Its no wonder that *melancholia*, what we today call depression, by the arrival of the 18th century had become epidemic. Without God's immanent presence, the world could be an anxious and lonely place.

The witch-craze was a done deal, dying out in a completely different age from when it appeared. People simply ceased to believe in witches. The Devil, the witch's purported ally, also, according to mechanistic thought, ceased to exist, corresponding with the final breakdown of the social network and taboos sustaining Devil beliefs. Of course, all kinds of Christian groups (as aforementioned, this Satan-based dualism was inherent to the Abrahamic lineages) would keep Devil beliefs going, but its day in court was done.

As the priest could no longer perform the magnitude of the miracles of the Mass, religion takes on a wholly new and reduced meaning. Cultivating a communally charged sacred space becomes a risky proposition. The need for catharsis, however, of course would not go away.

Throughout the Medieval and early Renaissance response to the Inquisition, people reportedly went into "spontaneous dance crazes." Bradford Keeney's *Shaking Medicine* (2007) thoroughly captures this movement:

> In the 1300s, so-called epidemics of wild religious dancing broke out in Europe, from the lower Rhine to the Netherlands and France. Hundreds, if not thousands, started dancing in the streets, in churches, in their homes, claiming to honor St. John. They would dance for hours and hours until they fell to the ground in shaking fits of ecstasy...In the 1400s, the wild dancing broke out again, this time called St. Vitus'dance.

If people weren't allowed to dance and celebrate life, the repressed body erupted anyway.

Culture would also increasingly reinvent new charismatic religious activity. In 17th century Europe the Quakers, Pietists, and Methodists promoted a fervent, emotional quality to their services. (The Quakers ultimately purged themselves of this cathartic component, and opted just for the silence.) And especially as Christianity moved into the Americas, evangelical expression would begin to restore what the Inquisition had taken away.

Perhaps the most globally influential response was when an enslaved, displaced African culture gets ahold of Christianity. The 18th and 19th century spirituals go on to inform popular musical movements (blues, jazz, rhythm 'n' blues, rock 'n' roll). A celebratory gospel experience also continues to deepen.

By the arrival of the 20th century, a secularized popular culture is making a downright commodity out of merry-making. Ritual starts to become a matter of choice, what one does with one's spare time. Capitalism provides the fuel for this new form of communitas.

A Capital Idea

The Protestant Reformation cannot entirely account for the rise of capitalism. However, it did remove the obstacles, the colluding powers of Church and feudal authorities, blocking the empowered emergence of an independent merchant middle class. The marriage of capitalism and a Protestant-based work ethic emerged from the Reformation, as Max Weber, the founder of modern sociology, directly unveiled in *The Protestant Ethic and the Spirit of Capitalism* (1958). In this light, the genesis of capitalism can be understood as a freedom movement. It was a way to get out from under the tyranny of feudalistic hierarchy and economy controlled by the noble class.

However, this new system of economics would now require raw resources to feed its factories. In terms of demographics and available resources, the European continent was stretched to the max. Thus, it was the land and resources of foreign, indigenous peoples that provided the impetus to colonize them. These people needed to be taught the values of World Four as well. The Worlds were in for a mighty collision.

Robert Boyle, 17th century chemist and governor of the colonial New England Company, wrote an essay entitled "Inquiry Into the Vulgarly Received Notion of Nature." He said, "The veneration wherewith men are imbued for what they call nature, has been a discouraging impediment to the empire of men over the inferior creatures of God." The creatures Boyle was referring to were the Native Americans his company was colonizing. They suffered from "their ridiculous Notions about the workings of Nature" and "the fond and superstitious practices those errors engaged themselves to" (Easlea 1980).

The internal side of this new socioeconomic and political equation looks like this. Nature had, for the first time in history, lost its primacy. The European mission to gain power over nature, to monitor, explain, exploit, and dominate nature's workings, went hand in hand with its capitalist driven imperialism. Manifest Destiny, a journalistic concept that showed up in the mid-19th century to justify the drive to conquer the American West, operated no differently. World Four was out to colonize all the Worlds that came before it.

The most drastic consequences, once again, however, are within. The intensities of the psyche are no longer siphoned off into the dramas of the myths, or an interactive God, but were now to abide by the austere asceticism of a Protestant derived worldview and work ethic. In essence, consciousness begins to flatten.

Pop Goes the Culture

Culture, in healthy and not always so healthy ways, would do much to compensate for this flattening. The imaginative powers of the psyche, the energetics of the body, yearn for an outlet. Most notable are the three-century-long traditions of Romanticism. Jean-Jacques Rousseau (1712-1778) is its original pioneer. Proposing "a theism of the heart," Rousseau launches beyond the Judeo-Christian lineage of World Four to romantically embrace the closeness with Nature the tribal mind seemed to possess. Rousseau was the first *wannabe* (...an Indian).

Throughout the 18th and 19th centuries, from the Europeans Goethe, Schiller, Blake, Wordsworth, Coleridge, Holderlin, and Keats to the Americans Emerson, Thoreau, and Whitman (just to name a few), World Four was rebelling from within. Visual art, music, dance, literature, poetry, philosophy, and various new religious possibilities (*i.e.*, New Thought Christianity) became independently distinct and vital expressions. The alienation that industrialization produces on the one hand, art, philosophy, and popular culture are soothing on the other. While embracing the individualist spirit that launches the modern age, there remains a deeper longing for connection and purpose.

As the Romantic Movement attends to the disenchantment of the educated classes, the arts of popular culture would provide its own therapeutic response to the lower classes. Much of the Western's celebratory activities become increasingly mass marketed, especially in the fields of music and dance. Staged operas and musical theaters in the 17th and 18th centuries become commonplace. The 19th century gives birth to the European cabaret and dance halls, while America is already capitalizing (*i.e.*, Stephen Foster) off of the musical legacy of its African populations.

At the turn of the 20th century, sheet music was the craze, then by the '20s, records; the '30s, radio; and the '40s, amplification. Rock 'n' roll, born in the '50s, split the culture wide open. Without necessarily saying much of anything at all, on a vibrational plane popular culture is providing cathartic release that the previous Worlds of myth and ritual had served.

John Trudell, a Sioux Indian and former spokesperson for the American Indian Movement, shared these thoughts in a rap song on growing up in America:

> Elvis showed us an out/ Something about him told us to be sensual is O.K./ We heard Elvis' song and for the first time we made up our minds/ We danced even if we didn't know how/ Even though he didn't know he said it, he showed it to us anyway/ And even though we didn't know we heard it,

we heard it anyway/ Man he woke us up. Look at the record/ Rock 'n' roll is based on revolution going way past 33-and-a-third/ Elvis was America's baby boomer Che/ I ought to know, I was in his army. (Trudell, "Baby Boom Che" in *AKA Graffiti Man*, 1992)

As Trudell shared in a personal interview, "Today the safest place to express truth is through art and culture because we live in a time when the institutions of the state don't tell the truth and everyone knows it. That's why creating art and culture is so important to our contribution and evolution as human beings. I started making music as a way to express truth." (John Trudell, *Santa Fe Sun*, 1995)

John Trudell

Today the safest place to express truth is through art and culture because we live in a time when the institutions of the state don't tell the truth and everyone knows it.

Over the course of the 20th century, pop music (be it, in rough chronological order: ragtime, jazz, blues, swing, gospel, rhythm 'n' blues, rock 'n' roll, soul, funk, reggae, rap, hip-hop, world beat, world music) creates one of the planet's most interconnecting and powerful rituals. It moves energy in the spine similar to the way ritual and spirit possession had done in ancient cultural practices.

Robbie Robertson, a rock star launching his career in the 1960s with The Band, and later musically paying homage to his Native American heritage, shared these thoughts with me in a personal interview:

> The musical world exists around going to a place and getting lost in the rhythms, getting lost in the beats, the dancing, the smoke. It is no different from what people have been doing for thousands of years. It is so strange when we think we're doing something so modern, and, in fact, it is so beautifully primitive. In the early days when I was working with

Robbie Robertson

It is about the unification of people through the music.

Bob Dylan and The Band, I played at Woodstock, at Watkins Glen, and the Isle of Wight. I played some of the biggest musical festivals ever on the planet, and they were about exactly what you're talking about, people gathering and feeling a togetherness. You go to an intertribal pow-wow and it is very similar. It is about the unification of people through the music. (1998)

Ritual rocks. It always did.

The Further Flattening of Consciousness

The dilemma is that all of the modern's new wonder toys, like first amplified music, radio and television, now computers, the internet, and virtual realities, can also serve to further flatten consciousness. The leaps of imagination required to enter into a poem, a novel, a meditation, the stories and old ways of indigenous culture, or direct conversations with nature herself, run the risk of being shortchanged by a surplus of already supplied imagery. The brain's thirst, the soul's longing, to actively imagine its own life risks becoming developmentally crippled.

Modern poet Robert Bly describes this as a deprivation of "mythopoetic consciousness." The following is an excerpt of a personal interview I conducted with Bly on this subject, published in the *Santa Fe Sun* in 1995:

> *Powell:* One of the things you address in your work is the loss of mythopoetic consciousness. This is not something just of the 20th century, but has been unfolding since the Renaissance. How do we introduce this, especially since we've lost it on such a vast scale?

> *Bly:* It's getting worse. There are more pure rationalists in the world. A lot of the younger ones that were more intuitive during the '60s have turned into Wall Street and academic types. There has been no need for rationalists, from their point of

view, to stretch themselves to understand what a myth is. People have been trained to believe that intuition and imagination is absurd, feminine, illogical, and wasteful.

Powell: What then do we do? One of the methods you talk about is mentoring and in some manner reconstructing initiation. Is this happening and is it working?

Bly: I think so. The old tradition is that learning is an interchange between two living people. As we know, with television and computers, there is less and less of that. In order for initiation to happen, you need grown men and women who are willing to devote a part of their lives to this, but I'm not sure if large numbers of them are going to show up.

Powell: To an extent, some of these principles have been borrowed by corporate America. Have you seen that in an effective way? Is there a certain risk to how has been used?

Bly: The corporate world of advertising co-opted a lot of the countercultural material that was brought forward during the 1960s. That was a disaster. And now the corporate world is co-opting a whole lot of material connected with self-advancement and self-growth. While some people can bridge these worlds, unless you're truly interested in soul, none of this is going to do any good. And most corporations are not interested in the soul. They want production.

With this rampant loss of formal rite of passage and the breakdown of family and community, it is a wonder that modern society manages to function at all. And yet it does, thanks to World Four's own particular adaptive use of ritual process.

Robert Bly

The old tradition is that learning is an interchange between two living people.

All Groan Up

Through millennia, each and every culture has provided our youth a mysterious threshold to battle and cross through into the equally mysterious land of adulthood. Girls were taught how to bleed into the earth, boys how to slay dragons. The psychic umbilical cords to Mom and Dad were cut. In the process, responsibilities and tasks were clearly defined. Society was sustained. Then the Industrial Revolution threw a wrench into this placid picture. Dad went off to work, mothers tended to hold onto their children more and/or, in their overwhelmed state, manage to neglect them. Lo and behold, families started to fall apart.

Children grew up with the ambivalent message of abandonment and suffocation and, no surprise, by the time teenage hormones hit, all hell broke loose. In less than three centuries Western

Culture has moved from a primarily agrarian based civilization to an industrialized one and now is being overhauled by what has been called and become the Information Age. The growing child, whose stability may have already been undermined by a broken family, also had little sense of community to fall back on in time of need and guidance.

The anthropological smokescreen is that there was never a truly established status quo definition of family to begin with. What we do know is that the agrarian extended family, which was just an addendum to the age-old societal wisdom that it takes a whole community to raise a child, collapses with the increasing advent of industrialized urbanization by the mid-18th century. A whole new developmental category would eventually be created, what we know as the *troubled* teenager. This phase can last well into one's forties and fifties. If there's no one, nothing, to grow us up, why should we?

Teenagers were troubled, foremost, because they had the liberty to be. It may appear that the loss of these more ancient cultural values, *i.e.*, the preeminence of family and God, has given way to a whole bunch of permissive calamities. However, it was also the transition from the stranglehold of an authoritarian feudal-based village society to one aiming towards capitalist values and democratic ideals that allowed all kinds of chaotic opportunities to enter the family picture. Creating an effective social maturation process was becoming increasingly elusive.

The surprise is not the alarming rate of dysfunctional families—the number of intact nuclear families has sunk to a staggering 25 percent (Kottak 2002), and who is to say how healthy those are—but that we have any measurable degree of functionality at all. This is the strange gift of World Four. While the breaking out of the stranglehold of feudal hierarchy and theological constraints still perpetuated similar injustices in a class entrenched capitalist society, there were new freedoms won as well. Most notable are the abilities to choose how one is to live one's life.

Individuation, once the cornerstone of the forager's Vision Quest, comes back from a long period of societal conformity (Worlds Two and Three) in a whole new fashion.

The older generation had certainly pretty well ruined this world before passing it on to us. But it is only a few years before the older people will step aside and let the world be run by those who those who see things as they are.

Such was the lament of F. Scott Fitzgerald in the 1920s, the crowning of the Jazz Age (in Powell 1995), who preceded by four decades the rebellious blast of trust that rocked the Flower Child 1960s generation. Despite the lack of coherent rite of passage, the youth instinctively create it for themselves. Once again, they don't always appear as the healthiest of choices. From all night raves to gang initiations, each new generation is creating new rituals and subcultures built around those rituals that have thrived since Fitzgerald and his peers partied in the Jazz Age. This is the way of the modern.

The Psychology of Everyday Life

This is the point. With each new possibility of dysfunction the breakdown of community and family has spawned, culture responds in immediate fashion to keep a semblance of order and balance going. Indeed, like the Worlds before it, World Four becomes swiftly adept at compensating for what it has lost. This is its magic.

When industrialization created the need for a steady work force, institutions appeared that supported family preservation. When France was establishing overseas colonies, family-centered philanthropic societies became common. Child rearing became the concern not only of physicians and educators but also of politicians. (Easlea 1980)

Mandatory education and helping profession agencies are created to help keep the family afloat. Public school systems and the monitoring eyes of professional psychology become World Four's regulatory rite of passage.

As a result, in the 21st century, World Four has produced a thoroughly psychologized culture. Expressing one's self, sharing one's feelings, getting in touch with your inner child, and becoming aware of self-defeating and co-dependent patterns are all examples of the spread of pop psychology inundating the modern sensibility. Any act of dysfunction produced by our cultural left hand is met by the right's hand immersion in being able to talk about and process it.

Tune into daytime television talk shows and you will get an immediate sense of this. The calamities infiltrating us modern individuals and families, the emotionally cathartic responses and subsequent therapeutic suggestions, are regularly hung out in public for the world to see. We have become thoroughly verse in discussing our dysfunctional dramas.

As a global family, we are all gaining increasing access to the psychological principles and support resources to help us to then deal with the kinds of drama (and trauma) the modern world creates. The summation of the contents of the life of the modern can then be seen by how one "manages" dysfunctions. We all have a vast selection of communitas experiences and therapeutic approaches to choose from to help us compensate and cope.

The Psychology of World Four

What then is the psychological shift from World Three to World Four? In the previous world of agrarian, feudal hierarchies, the archetypal realities of the collective unconscious were what St. Augustine of the early Christian Church termed *memoria*. Everything was, in some manner, a reflection of God. The collective unconscious was more attuned to a divine consciousness than the modern but, at the same time, considerably more regulated through the confines of theocracy. We see, for instance, these spiritual depths in the Islamic psyche coincide with cultural and individual repression. Theocracy produces spiritually deep and pure experience. But it can also be rather confining.

In World Four, psychology comes to the rescue. Freud and Jung, through the psychoanalytic investigation of what is now being called the *unconscious*, find a new way of addressing this ancient territory. James Hillman, a renegade Jungian (as most Jungians are), shares the particular nature of this exploration:

> The concept of the unconscious was already "topical" around 1800 and fashionable by 1870, but the unconscious was in fact a palace left from antiquity and the Renaissance, still inhabited by the surviving pagan Gods and once called the realm of "memoria." But now, whereas memoria had the reality of a fundamental power of the soul and needed no empirical proof, the modern's evidence for the unconscious has been by negative demonstration through its disturbing effects upon ego consciousness: slips of the tongue, forgetting, complex indicators, hysterical symptoms, multiple personality (etc.). Our modern evidence for memoria has been drawn from psychopathology! We have had to be sick to rediscover in felt experience the power of this imaginal faculty. (Hillman 1972)

This phenomenon, of course, is nothing new. The difference is that whereas in shamanic (Worlds One and Two) and ancient culture (World Three) illness was the doorway into the deeper language of the soul, modern psychology begins with the premise that there is something wrong.

In short, the emergence of psychoanalysis replaced God (memoria) with the notion of the unconscious. Freud was mechanistic in his analysis of the psyche. Deities were projections of wanting a bigger and better mother and father, a way of working out our basic needs on a cultural scale. The risk is this:

For centuries, people have experienced various utterly convincing visions, sounds, and smells, the reality of which did not depend upon the sole correspondence with an outer object. Some cultures encourage and expect these events; they are necessary for initiation.... But now the demon and ghost are banished, but with them go the ancestor and the angel; they enter the realm of psychopathology. (Hillman 1975)

The human species has always had a difficult time handling the contents of its own psyche. In previous Worlds, that tension was siphoned off through myth and ritual and interactive dialogues with various kinds of Creators. In World Four, psychology begins to come to the fore, a discipline whose language is couched in pathology.

The human journey is now considered treatable by a wide range of therapeutic options. The more extreme cases are offered asylum, a practice that dates back to the late Middle Ages. While medical science's prototypical doctor, Paracelsus (1493-1541), advocated a kind of psychotherapy for treatment of the insane, the English psychiatrist Walter Cooper Dendy first introduced the term *psychotherapeia* in 1853. A little more than a century later, and there were over sixty officially sanctioned forms of psychotherapy, and countless others types of treatment considered more alternative.

The nature of these therapies falls in line with the principles of the Medicine Wheel as introduced in World One. Behavioral therapies are in the South (Body), Psychodynamic and Gestalt in the West (Heart), Cognitive to the North (Mind), and Archetypal, Transpersonal and Humanistic in the East. Cognitive-behavioral, the north-south poles, aim for immediate visible changes, and thus most appealing to the modern's solution oriented societies. They provide the anchor by which we learn to become responsible citizens.

The West/East poles—the matters of the heart and working out the shadow sides of one's archetypal endowment—are, however, not so quickly fixed. Indeed, it takes the journey of a lifetime for these dimensions to fully heal and mature. These dimensions don't, however, have easily measurable outcomes, and thus are not as accessible for public funding.

In the course of the last fifty years, an increasing number have also been prescribed psychiatric drugs. Anti-depressants, anti-anxiety and sleep meds, attention deficit disorder medications, etc. become a new kind of status quo. As in the previous Worlds, the psyche is seeking to be rebalanced. While clearly assisting people who are suffering, there is the risk of a biological determinism here that the psyche is considered as nothing more than chemically ordered parts.

> Our psychological language parallels the industrial revolution, positivism, nationalism, secularism, and all that is characterized as the "nineteenth-century mind." Our language represents more specifically the academic and medical mind of the nineteenth century. Psychology and psychopathology are children of the late Enlightenment, the hopeful Age of Reason as it hardened into an Age of Matter.... The ruling psychologies of the Enlightenment, from Locke through Freud declare the soul to be empty of imaginal remembrance.... The mind is a "tabula rasa" (blank slate), it consists only in will and learning... The imaginal memory is not considered an authentic region of the soul. (Hillman 1975)

The contents of the psyche become less important than the ability to maneuver through those contents and maintain a (relatively speaking) competent social functioning.

There's Nothing New about the New Age

Pretty strident stuff, and certainly much of humanistic psychology (*i.e.*, Carl Rogers, Abraham Maslow), and transpersonal / anthropology (*i.e.*, a vast array of Jungians, Marion Woodman and Robert Johnson two of the more prominent) has served to counterbalance this. But when the rubber hits the road, when the dollar crunch masterminds how it is that mental health issues need to be addressed, treated, written, and talked about, the "scientifically-based" cognitive-behavioral paradigm is still what comes to the fore. As I worked for years in agencies for Native American and agrarian Hispanic clients, their solution-oriented treatments do not necessarily address the disjointedness these cultures (or many of the rest of us) feel beyond the scientific trajectory of the modern's sensibility and therapeutic modalities.

The implication is that the modern world is somehow less spiritual than these older ones. This may not be altogether true. The spiritual simply becomes more individualized, or as many a modern might respond to this subject, "I'm spiritual, not religious." This orientation refers to a whole other kind of outlook, a New Age blending that, like modern psychology, also came into being in the late 19th century. Madame Blavatsky's theosophical application of Hindu principles to all of the world's teachers suggested that spiritual Masters will readily begin to show up in our lives and psyche (the outer and inner planes) when we are ready for them and consciously call them in.

This unprecedented celebration of all of the planet's wisdom traditions found concrete representation in Chicago's 1893 Parliament of World Religions. Respectively representing the crowning points of Western and Eastern thought, Mary Baker Eddy (founder of Christian Science) and Swami Vivekananda (Yogananda's teacher) were in attendance. As Vivekananda stated to a rousing ovation,

> Sectarianism, bigotry, and its horrible descendant, fanaticism, have long possessed this beautiful Earth. They have filled the earth with violence, drenched it often with human blood, destroyed civilization, and sent whole nations to despair. Had it not been for these horrible demons, human society would be far more advanced than it is now.
> (Swami Vivekananda speech at the World Congress of Religions September 11, 1893, www.swamij.com)

For many a modern, one's spiritual life became a matter of sifting through and picking out the best of all Worlds. The risks have been a spiritual supermarket dilution of these traditions. The benefits have been a truly global integration that invites in the Fifth World.

The final piece of the modern outlook is an increasing agnosticism, which also has its roots in older Worlds (Greek rationalism, Buddhism's non-theistic approach). This can run the spectrum from secular humanism to a cynically driven hedonism. However, as the master of Comparative Religion, Mircea Eliade, stated thirty years ago, it is questionable whether the sacred dimension can ever just go away. The psyche will not allow for it.

> There are those in Western society who want to be, and declare themselves to be areligious. On the level of everyday consciousness, they are perhaps right; but they continue to participate in the sacred through dreams and daydreams, through certain attitudes, through distractions, through nostalgias and impulses. Religion may have been "forgotten," but the sacred survives, buried in the unconscious. (Eliade 1978)

How this "buried" sacred continues to pop up in the context of World Four, of the modern world, will be addressed in the remainder of this chapter.

⏯ Culture of the American Southwest
The Anglos World Four Arrives Full-Tilt Boogie

In the Southwest, the Americans were as much a shock to the Spanish as the Spanish were to the indigenous peoples. Up until the 1820s, the Americans were forbidden from entering the territory. This was a fragile frontier, technically owned by the King of Spain, and the Spanish considered the Americans a threat. They were right.

Mountain man Zebulon Pike got arrested trapping furs and was shipped off to lovely Chihuahua. But finally, like the American Revolution, New Spain got defeated from within. Mexico, twice the size it is now, comes into being. That same year, 1821, American traders were invited in via what becomes the Santa Fe Trail. People were thrilled to get the new technologies coming out of the States. Within a decade, with this new breed of culture, all the furs of the Sangre de Cristo mountains were trapped out and the herds of deer and elk depleted. The entrepreneurial spirit of World Four had arrived.

While the Americans eventually took over the territory in the 1840s, the full impact of their industrial culture did not hit until the arrival of the railroads in 1880. Within ten years, the number of banks jumped from two to fifty. A new ethic and value system had landed, a jarring clash of capitalist versus community values. On a parallel track, an 1883 piece of legislation known as the "Courts of Indian offenses" referred to Indian rites and customs as "barbarous." The medicine man was made a criminal.

This antagonism increased up until the 1920s when Commissioner of Indian Affairs Charles Burke sent a letter "to all Indians" urging them to give up dances and ceremonies voluntarily or he would be forced "to issue an order against these useless and harmful performances" (Utter, *American Indians*, 1993). In that same decade there was another piece of legislation up before the Congress, the Bursum Bill, that would have stripped away the last protection there was for Pueblo Indians to remain sovereign proprietors of their own land and resources.

And, as already discussed, by the turn of the century 80 percent of the Spanish land grants ended up in the hands of Anglo-American lawyers and settlers. Further, with the 1906 launching of the National Forest system, more and more land used by both the Native and Spanish peoples was slipping out of their hands. Without land, without infrastructure, these cultures were brought to their knees. "Inquisition Number Two" had arrived.

Religious Freedom for Whom?

The irony is that for a country founded on the principles of religious and cultural toleration, the Spanish and the Native would not receive those benefits. Despite all of their democratic ideals, the industrialized peoples were largely unaware of their own ethnocentric blinders. The democratic freedom pronounced by the founders of the American nation was only for those of their own industrialized World Four.

> The cultures of the Indians and the Spaniards, frozen in a "fixed, traditional present," were no match for the Americans, and by the 1800s the Spaniards had gone from being conquistadores to being "conquistados" and had joined the ranks of the superseded Indians. The Anglos brought with them a mind-set that had not been seen in these parts before: the analytic curiosity of the Enlightenment. Nature was to be dissected, collected, categorized, catalogued, manipulated, and conquered, rather than respected and revered and let be. (Shoumatoff, *Legends of the American Desert*, 1997)

If it had been given full rein, industrial culture could have wiped out the essence of what these older cultures were about. The beginnings of the World Five, however, were also arriving. As usual, the revolution began from within.

At the turn of the 20th century, another type of Anglo started to show up. As artists, anthropologists and wayward travelers, this was a group seeking a kind of disenfranchising from their own culture. Through their political awareness and savvy, they publicized and brought down the draconian legislation that could have meant an end to the Southwest's land-based cultures. These were, in other words, the first wannabes. Or, as a Pueblo friend of mine kindly said to me, "You're not a wannabe, you're a should-have-been."

While the fight was political and external, what these new Anglos were truly seeking was an internal restoration of the psyche that, for them, the industrial world had stripped away.

In the years preceding and then following World War I a longing developed among Anglo Americans for the simpler times of preindustrial America: The nation had, some held, grown too fast, had lost something in the process; and now there was a yearning to return to that fast disappearing life on the soil. The ancient cultures of the Native American and Hispanic peoples yet thriving on the lands of the twentieth century Southwest, where "tradition and rootedness were life's primary treasures," seemed to offer a sanctuary to Anglo American pilgrims who sought a lifestyle beyond the rigid grasp of industrialized, urbanized America. In the first decades of this century, Anglo expatriates from Boston, New York, and Chicago flocked to New Mexico not to conquer or reform, not to "tame" the indigenous cultures and native traditions, but through observation and exposure, to reinvent their own. After centuries as the destination of conquerors, New Mexico became the destination for those who felt they had been conquered by their own societies. (Poling-Kempes, *Valley of Shining Stone*, 1997)

This was a wave of American counterculture trying to go back in time as a hope and way of reinventing themselves. Seventy some years later (1975 to be exact) I arrived at the tail end of another wave.

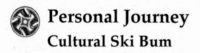 ## Personal Journey
Cultural Ski Bum

Within a week of my arrival into New Mexico, I was renting a room from an Apache Indian. I had been in school for a year studying cultural anthropology but had decided at that point I'd much rather be a cultural ski bum. And Taos was the perfect place to accomplish that. When in high school there was a movie, *Easy Rider*, partially shot in the Taos area, perfectly capturing that era. Starring Peter Fonda, Dennis Hopper, and a young Jack Nicholson, my parents would not let me see it. They were afraid that, like my two older brothers, my life would be swept away by this bold and reckless counterculture. They were right.

After another week, the Apache man came home with a Pueblo Indian and Dennis Hopper, who would go on to play some version of his crazed self in a full and varied Hollywood acting career. (At the time Hopper also seemed to have a bit of a drug problem and was rather adept at making people angry.) Somewhere late into that night I made the mistake of complementing the handmade beautifully desert-dyed, silver buckle belt with coral and turquoise inlay of that Pueblo Indian. He took it off and gave it to me. Considering all that these peoples had been through at the hands of the Europeans, and that I was unmistakably White, this was an indication of how deeply ingrained the values of selflessness and generosity were still built into tribal cultures. They had their limits, too, of course. History demanded such.

Because of what came down historically, namely the Inquisition, and then with the arrival of the Americans, Inquisition Number Two, the tribes are understandably reluctant to share what is more meaningful to them and their ritual activity. They've gone underground. There were many times when I was working on the Pueblos when I was told not to come to work. I knew what they were doing. They knew I knew what they were doing. But, we didn't talk about it. Ask a four-year-old Pueblo child about ceremony and you get a very stoic, silent four-year-old.

Another reason, one that addresses the true depths of these cultures, is that this is esoteric stuff and you don't give out the gold—that is, the knowledge—so easily. You have to earn it. While anthropologists are used to researching everything they want to know, in indigenous culture knowledge comes in pieces; the rites of passages of one's life. It is not until one is an elder that all of the pieces of the puzzle come together.

As admonished by the Navajo Peyote Medicine Man I thought I would write about some day (which I now am), "Go study your own tribal roots. Don't take mine." The Anglos were drawn to the

American Southwest by the sense that there was some missing piece of themselves that could be restored by interaction with the Native cultures. Yes, there are missing pieces. But, the restoration for World Four begins and ends within. This is what I discovered.

At the base of the Germanic psyche, at the base of my heritage, is a Norse God named Wotan. He was the Dionysus, the Shiva, of the North. Thor is his cultural cousin. Zeus and Yahweh are not too distantly related. There is a fierce masculine quality about all of them, so they are to be approached with caution. When aligned with him, Wotan had a whole lot of juice to give you.

When Christianity—World Three—worked its way north, Wotan, like many of the pagan Gods encountered by this Abraham-ic faith, went under and became portrayed as the Devil. Wotan was not too happy about this and, like Gods and Goddesses are prone to do, continued to linger in the psyche as an archetypal force. Switch to World Four. Germany is defeated in World War I and further hu-miliated by the economic deprivation to follow. The thinly placed veil of Christianity gets torn off. Wotan comes roaring back.

As Jung noted in his analysis of post World War II Nazis, Wotan was a figure that still kept showing up in people's dreams. He was an active force. Without him, Hitler would have had no psychic energy to coalesce and catalyze. And, as are the tragic con-sequences of archetypal forces when repressed and ignored, they can come out in all too dark and shadowy ways. Wotan, once the projected Devil, turns around and puts the same projection onto the Jews and the Western world. As so often in the tides of history, the oppressed becomes the oppressor.

My grandfather, fluent in German and the son of a Baptist preacher, was of the Nazi generation. Though as second generation he was Americanized, he carried within him a kind of angst that characterized his distant ancestors and relatives. This same angst—what modern psychiatry might diagnose as depression, anxiety disorder, or bipolar—runs throughout our family.

This was an angst described in the Bible as "the sins of the fathers" that were passed down through the generations. What, then, is this angst about? A dream helped me. My grandfather was drowning. I dove in to save him. I found out in my rescue that the reason why he was drowning is that he had lost his faith. Indeed, this had happened in real life. He had left his father's church, which was nearly heretic in those days. My great-grandfather, according to my grandfather, had come to forgive him, because his son had come to find a similar reverence in and with nature.

This reverence blended well with my grandfather's fondness for the Transcendentalists Emerson and Thoreau. Indeed, my grandfather would revere and study the Seneca Indian. His land was a part of the Seneca lands they considered their sacred birthplace. In his own way, my Grandfather had become a kind of a wannabe, and he had inadvertently taught a few of us grandchildren to do the same.

The Fifth World is just around the corner and demanding we each open up to our ancestral possibilities. There is still ancestral work left to complete. Wotan and these old shamanic Gods, for whatever belligerent force they might have been in history, did not start out as such, and are now seeking a kind of redemption. They are not about to go away. Nor are our angers or fears, but all aspects of the psyche can be transformed. That dynamic is what the following dream captured:

I was at a rollerblade/skateboard park, a sustained penchant for adolescents for the last several decades. Many of them were sprawled out on the floor bleeding profusely from their search for thrills. Their quest was for some kind of meaningful transcendent consciousness, a rite of passage, amidst a mainstream culture fairly barren of such. At this point Wilbert Alix saunters into the dream, a self-professed modern day shaman whom I had met at an Altered States of Consciousness conference in October 2003 in Albuquerque, New Mexico.

Trained in what is termed a "neo-shamanic" trance-dance rite of passage experience, Alix essentially brings the energy and musical styles of a rave, an all night party, to a more pronounced ritual setting. Alix considers this the high-octane approach to higher consciousness. In the dream, Alix picks me up and holds me horizontally around his waist and is about to start spinning to induce my own transcendent experience. I exclaim we are going to do this amidst this bloody carnage and he replies, "That is how rite of passage is these days."

The dream then sequences into a conversation with a bitter Native American women and performer who is acrimoniously denouncing her Native American performer husband (who fails to show up for gigs) as "a lazy-ass Capricorn." As that husband, and in real life the Capricorn that I am, I step back, meditate upon my response, and then calmly suggest to the woman that "Capricorn is Christ energy, which, in Native spirituality, can be thought of as *compassion.*"

The masculine has let the feminine down. The true and noble warrior is missing. In this dream, the healing comes through as the Christ. The very archetype used to oppress this indigenous layer of the psyche and culture is reconfigured and reclaimed as a healing force. The colonized, as has often been the case in history, become more rooted in the Christ than the Christians who colonized them.

In one mere dream, the nearly complete verticality of developmental psychology, from adolescence to late adulthood, and evolutionary anthropology, from shamanism to Christ energy to modern day rite of passage, is unveiled. The male adolescent, in the perilous attempt to find the inner self (through skateboarding), is tragically wounded instead, resulting in all kinds of despair and identity diffusion. Having not survived this rite of passage entirely in tact can incur bouts of isolation and depression.

The Native American woman then shows up and, while making her living as a performer, the male side can't show up, as has happened so rampantly in abused indigenous and colonized cultures. The masculine energy becomes errant, stagnant, and sometimes violent. The masculine becomes emasculated. And thus the considerable tension with the feminine. She wants and deserves a reliable mate, but she also must understand the masculine as an emasculated warrior and provider in order to recover and heal from this loss. The masculine has a hard time showing up. Still does.

The young people of World Four lack coherent rite of passage. They often provide for themselves tortuous substitutes (thrill seeking, piercings, etc.). The Penitentes of New Mexico's World Three flagellated themselves in a similar manner as a way to viscerally feel and display their pain. The Native cultures of Worlds One and Two have had many of their rites of passage pulled out from under them. And those rites that are left may not necessarily address and release the kinds of pressures induced by the ways of the modern world.

The point is that regardless of what our backgrounds are, at this time on the planet we are now being asked to recognize and reconcile the clash of archetypes from all the Worlds. This freedom of choice is what World Four afforded, but it is World Five that will give us the skills to allow this to come about.

⌻ Practical Applications

There is no culture or individual untouched by the industrial world. Its spread, the pull, is too great. While, ironically, World Four promotes the opportunities for grabbing one's glories, for most on the planet security gets pulled out from under us. The psyche suffers tremendous anxiety as a result. Whereas World Three potentially presents an increasing stranglehold on one's freedom, like in Worlds One and Two, the individual was foremost identified and supported by their community. In World Four, the individual is left all alone.

What then shows up in my psychotherapist office are a lot of anxiety disorders, depression and addictions. Loneliness and insecurity are no fun. For those from World One through Three, World Four seems like a rude assault. A lack of caring glares through all of capitalism's promises. Extended dysfunctional families and tribes, contradictions in terms, become the order of the day. No traditional social structure can withstand the imperative of the "almighty dollar." The freedoms World Four proposes may seem rather empty.

The challenge and redemption that World Four holds is that arena of *choice* despite the losses. For most of us, from all of the Worlds, this means how to go about repairing and restoring family and community. This may entail starting from scratch, salvaging what one can, and recreating family and community in whatever form possible. World Four presents every kind of support group imaginable.

Therapeutic applications include the more modern domains of counseling psychology. This often involves an exploration of how one's own family of origin has set the stage for a kind of a wounding, and then path out of that wounding, that many of us modern folk have felt. Again, this is not about blame or shame, but the recognition that whatever one's story is around family of origin, this is a reflection of both the dysfunction and opportunity that World Four created.

For those of us born into this world, which really means just about everybody, there can be a tension with the vast array of choices. The challenge is finding clarity and stable means of support throughout this process of finding one's voice and way in the world. There is also the realizing and accepting of one's limitations.

Psychologically, World Four tends to be the most treacherous of all. The individual must rely on him/herself in ways that formerly family, community, and religion (however fixed) took care of. There is a lot more opportunity, even among the various relationships and groups one is involved in, to feel alone and unsupported.

Relatively speaking, this World has been on the planet a short time: a mere five hundred years. World Four seems to be an intense preparatory period for the World to come. The upside is we have become a highly psychological global community. This is World Four's religion. As we learn to navigate the pitfalls of society and our psyche, we learn the skills to restore what has been lost to us.

Indigenous groups are now coming together and revitalizing themselves in unprecedented ways. The free will that World Four affords allows the choice to re-enter one's own traditions by choice, not coercion. Meanwhile, many of the modern seek the indigenous. All sorts of contemporary psychological and wellness techniques, from contemplative traditions to alternative medicine to simply making physical health and time with nature a priority, have become huge commodities. In a strange posture, capitalism heals itself by sifting, from the rubble of the cultures it has threatened, their healing features. We are becoming multicultural, intercommunicative global citizenry. We can't help but arrive at World Five.

An elderly man I came into contact with in the context of a men's network (The Mankind Project) shared his story with me. He had been diagnosed with an inoperable prostate tumor. Diseases of the prostate have become epidemic for men in World Four. It is the site of what the Hindu perspective and Ayurvedic medicine designates as the first *chakra*. Known as the Muladhara or *root chakra*, this is about our sheer security and survival in the world.

While World Four has fostered the possibility of extravagant lifestyles, we also fear this could be pulled out from under us at any time. This is especially true of men, who have been culturally raised to be the breadwinners. The traditional security blanket of family and community has been stripped away.

Living in the American Southwest, the man had the option of going to see a medicine man from a nearby indigenous culture. Though not particularly aware of or in tune with the principles of this type of culture, he figured what did he have to lose. The medicine man suggested he give this tumor a name and begin to dialogue with it. This is what modern psychology calls visualization and *active imagination*. The fruits of the Worlds intermingle.

The name he gave that tumor was "activity." This was a man recently retired and perplexed by what to do with so much time in his life and psyche. He was, in truth, terrified by no longer having the distraction of his working life to separate him from the thoughts of his final days and death.

The man did some sweat lodges to cleanse himself of the toxicity and the fear he had around this subject. The medicine was to get in touch with and dialogue with the energetic that would have caused such a tumor. The tumor began to shrink. Seven years later, he was standing before me telling his story.

As has been a persistent theme through all of these Worlds, World Four provides the antidote to itself. Preoccupied with money and security and grabbing all of the gusto one can by mid-life generally becomes a hollow and exhausting pursuit. Though living longer lives, with the pace of modern life it can still feel like we are in a hurry to die. What I offer to my World Four clients (which, by definition, means all of them) is what I continuously attempt to give myself: inroads back into human *being*, not just human *doing*. Worlds One, Two and Three carry many of those roads. World Five is the integration.

World Four Summary

World Four is about the advent of industrial culture and the modern mind. Much of the hierarchal injustices that the feudalism of World Three created were further perpetuated by the capitalism of World Four. The greatest movements of death (Inquisition, 20th century holocausts) and liberation (freedom of slaves, women's movement, civil rights) are introduced in the same World. The fruition of this world is being able to freely choose how to live one's life.

For better and worse, the planet, through this colonial expansion, became one world. Much of the oppression that happened played itself out along ethnic and racial demarcations. For a society to step towards true democracy, it is this wounding and restoration that still must be addressed. Where World Four needs the most internal attention is in the breakdown of family and community and the stresses this has put on the growing child and individual.

Global Archetypal Unfolding
Liberation and Death

The modern world begins with the paradox of democratic ideals and the first holocausts (Crusade, Inquisition) the planet had ever known. Cultures are threatened or lost by the imperialism that World Four creates, while at the same time there are global liberation movements addressing inequalities in gender, class, ethnicity and race.

Downsizing the Imagination

A trio of distinct movements—Humanism, Neoplatonism, and Rationalism—both complement and come into conflict with one another in medieval Europe. Eventually the *rationalist paradigm* will take hold as the central one, putting at risk other elements of culture, including all of the previous Worlds.

225

Neoplatonism

The scientific revolution, contrary to modern myth, is not a progression from superstition to reason, but rather is based on a reappropriation of ancient knowledge (Greek, Egyptian, Arabic) that then must fit within the confines of Europe's Inquisitional Order. These Neoplatonic movements included alchemy, Hermeticism, and the Kabbalah. The Rosicrucians and Freemasons would adopt some of this wisdom.

Crazed about Witches

The witch-craze heightened, rather than diminished, with the arrival of the Renaissance (16th and 17th centuries). This produced a pronounced conflict with Europe's World Three hierarchal interests and an older World Two village-based cosmology where, notably, women had more power.

The Mechanical Philosophy

The tension between the World Three hierarchies of Church and Nobility versus the Neoplatonist movements and World Two level culture led to a whole new paradigm. The mechanical philosophy incorporates the fruits of this tension, a rigorous experiment based empiricism, but strips science of its rich metaphysical foundation.

A Capital Idea

Capitalism begins as the liberation movement of an independent merchant middle class to get out from under the economic tyranny of feudalism. Over time it mixes in with the individualized self-sacrificing ethic produced by the Protestant Reformation. When capitalism requires raw resources to keep feeding its production, this ethic becomes the colonizing force (Manifest Destiny) by which many of the planet's cultures are subdued.

Pop Goes the Culture

While the Inquisition and Protestant Reformation had eliminated many of the more celebratory aspects of religious and social life, popular culture wouldn't stand for it and came roaring back in the 18th, 19th and 20th centuries with all kinds of aesthetic forms (music, dance, visual art, literature, poetry and philosophy) as a means of compensating for this "loss of soul."

The Further Flattening of Consciousness

The modern world's new technologies, while accelerating the interconnection of all of the world's cultures, also poses the risk of a "dulling" cultural expression where people cannot readily access the *mythopoetic consciousness* that centrally characterized Worlds One, Two, and Three.

All Groan Up

World Four eliminates the cohesive rites of passage that propelled the earlier Worlds, particularly for adolescents. However, as each succeeding modern generation has demonstrated, through subcultural language and ritual, young people will manifest their own thresholds to step through so as to better know their identity in a complex, fragmented modern world.

The Psychology of Everyday Life

The budding discipline of psychology would provide the impetus for social agencies and the helping professions to guide and set boundaries for its cultural constituents. Formerly the responsibility of clergy and shamans, this new paradigm emphasized a cognitive/behavioral approach that the humanistic and transpersonal movements psychology attempts to balance out.

The Psychology of World Four

The discipline of psychology, based largely on the medical model, addresses the psyche in terms of pathology. While pathology certainly exists, this paradigm limits the nature of the *soul journey* that the earlier cultural Worlds conceived of as a natural part of life's challenges. Over time, other movements in psychology compensate for this, creating its own medicine wheel array of perspectives (South/Body—Behavioral; West/Heart—Psychodynamic/Gestalt; North/Mind—Cognitive; East/Spirit—Archetypal, Transpersonal, Humanistic).

There's Nothing New about the New Age

World Four's separation of Church and State allow for an influx of spiritual possibilities, including the choice to not be spiritual at all. Some moderns start mixing and matching portions from all of the world religions and wisdom traditions, which generically is referred to as the New Age. The notion "spiritual but not religious" becomes its own kind of religion.

⫸ Culture of the American Southwest
The Anglo World Four Arrives Full-Tilt Boogie

The capitalist drive behind the American push westward severely impacts the survival of the indigenous (Athabaskan, Puebloan) and agrarian cultures (Hispano) of the Southwest.

Religious Freedom for Whom?

While based on the notion of religious toleration, legislation that the United States government tries to pass and enforce threatens to put an end to the land-based cultures of the Southwest. The notion of democratic freedom, created by World Four, only seemed to apply to those cultures that were of World Four. Everyone else needed to be civilized. A new type of Anglo (artists, anthropologists) showing up in the late 19th century, who themselves felt disenfranchised from their own culture, help put an end to that legislation. They, however, couldn't help but bring their own cultural baggage.

✿ Personal Journey
Cultural Ski Bum

I arrived in the mid-1970s as part of one more wave of searching Anglos. The older cultures both resented and began to adopt the ways introduced by the increasing influx of industrial culture.

⬜ Practical Applications

We are all bound by World Four, a cultural uprootedness matched by a rapid-fire technology and information network that allows other forms of connectedness to happen. The helping professions are overloaded with helping others, as they try to help themselves, in finding a balance amidst the cacophony.

POST-APOCALYPTIC
THINKING

WORLD FIVE
Coming of Age in a World Without Borders

CONTEMPLATIVE

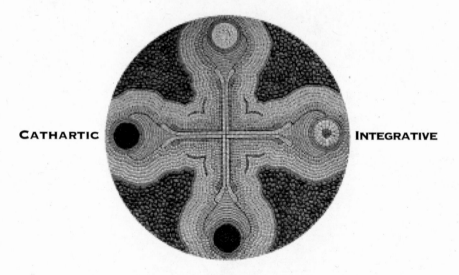

CATHARTIC

INTEGRATIVE

TANTRIC
(EMBODIED)

First Onset:

21ST CENTURY

Predominant Infrastructure:

PARTIAL BREAKDOWN OF INTERNATIONAL INDUSTRIAL ECONOMY,
REVITALIZING OF REGIONAL AND LOCAL SUBSISTENCE ECONOMIES

Predominant Social Structure:

CREATING AND RECREATING FAMILY AND CULTURE AS NEEDED

Predominant Superstructure:

ARCHETYPAL DIALOGUES WITH GOD

Predominant Medicinal Response:

WORLD MEDICAL SYSTEM

Predominant Mode of Thinking:

HOLISTIC, INTEGRATIVE

Human Potential Advance:

NON-ETHNOCENTRIC CULTURAL RELATIVISM, PEACE

Shadow Sides:

DILUTION OF GLOBAL WISDOM TRADITIONS

American Southwest Culture:

WORLD FIVE MECCA

Personal Journey:

LETTING GO OF BITTERNESS AND SORROW

Global Archetypal Unfolding
The Future Was Yesterday

World Five is not *coming*. It is not some romanticized New Age hope. World Five is already live and kicking. It can be seen, foremost, in the increasing multicultural spread that has inundated our daily lives and contacts. We have become a planet of immigrants on the move, a world, culturally speaking, without borders.

As has been the anthropological pattern, the prospects of the next World show up in the seeds of the previous ones. However now tainted by the imperialist demands of capitalism and the ethnocentric blinders of colonialism, World Four started as a movement of freedom from the harsh constraints of feudalistic theocracy. Those freedom plans still await their fruition, but mighty seeds are planted. In the 12th century, the poet Rumi forecast a global awakening:

> I look not at the tongue and the speech; I look at the inward spirit and the state of feeling ... I want burning, burning: become friendly with that burning! Light up a fire of love in thy soul, burn thought and expression entirely away! Oh Moses, they that know the conventions are of one sort, they whose souls and spirits burn are of another sort. (Noss, *A History of the World's Religions*, 2007)

As the Spanish philosopher-poet Ibn al-'Arabi shared a century earlier,

> There was a time, when I blamed my companion if his religion did not resemble mine; Now, however, my heart accepts every form.... Love alone is my religion. (Noss 2007)

The point is not to water down these wisdom traditions into one New Age global mish-mash. Instead, the quest is to deepen in our tracks, to put together the evolutionary quest for consciousness as a giant interlocking jigsaw puzzle.

Sikhism, one of the last world religions to emerge, was born in the 16th century. Now the planet's 5th largest, Sikhism boldly proposes this: there are many names for God, but in the final analysis, there is only one humanity. Subsequently, Europe's 17th century Rosicrucians laid out the blueprints for a divine global order. While received in this dawning of World Four's secular age as the impetus to democracy, an inspired ethical imperative would demand a return to consensual, rather than strictly hierarchal, means of governance. The glue to this newly proposed democracy was the belief that human thought had a divine core to it.

Whatever harsh landscapes the industrialization of the planet introduced, cultural movements were bound and determined to seek out a silver lining. The Romantic Movement starting in the 18th century and the Bahá'í and Theosophy faiths of the 19th century are further movements exploring the core wisdom that beckons to unite the species. And, for all of its bundles of contradiction, it was the social experiment of the United States of America toward which humanity would continue to turn its hopes.

The Great Awakenings

No matter how industrialized the outside culture is, dig deep enough into the psyche and the older layers of archetypes are still there. They surface when culture most needs them. There has been a triage of Great Awakenings that have descended upon American popular culture. The first, occurring from about 1720 to 1750, involved ecstatic whirling, spontaneous trance states, and being slain in the spirit. This was Christianity springing back from the repression of the Reformation, Counter-Reformation, and Inquisition. Out of that first Awakening came many of the ideals and drive leading to the American Revolution.

The second Awakening, taking place from the 1820s up until the Civil War, produced a whole new set of revivalist expressions, from the more conservative ranks of mainstream denominations to the left wing propositions of Christian socialism and Transcendentalism. America's freeing of the slaves and the suffragette movement would be the beneficial results.

We are now in the tail end of a third Awakening, a movement originating with the spiritualized pop culture explosion of the 1960s and a more humanistic, transpersonal slant on human psychology. This has been called generically the New Age and, foremost, is showing up in people's lives as integrative medicine. All of the planet's healing modalities, past and present, are virtually at our disposal.

The threefold Awakening process linking these Awakenings remains the same throughout. At the bottom floor is the primal quest, the **shamanic**, to connect and interconnect. Sound, movement, rhythm, trance, telepathy are the primary ingredients. The next floor of the psyche, the **ancient**, holds forth the compassion-filled archetypes of the world religions—Christ, Buddha, etc. This is the compassion-based consciousness of the axial period of history, the thousand years leading up to and including Christ, brought to fruition. The contemplative traditions of prayer and meditation are the fruits.

And finally, the **modern** realm, the discerning ability to sift back through the shortsighted positivism (what you see is what you get) of its own era into a modern appropriation of these older traditions. The Fifth World is crying out for the integration of *the shamanic, the ancient, the modern—the tribal, the agrarian, the industrial*—a quest to make humanity **whole from within.**

The common denominator threading this evolution of humanity's soul is this:

How we bear our pain may have a great deal to do with what kind of soul work we have done during our life. It also suggests that relating at a soul level to those who suffer pain (including ourselves)—grieving, mourning, crying, not for but with the suffering—may be as important as the technical measures we employ to alleviate pain. Such engagement also allows for the expression of the soul that may have been neglected for years—the sorrows, regrets, unlived hopes and dreams, desires, unresolved conflicts, misunderstandings, and most important, all the fears that still linger and become intensified when confronted with our mortality. We are able to be of service to those who suffer only to the extent that we have been able to transform fear in our own lives.... The shift begins when our encounters with fear go from being a burden to becoming a means through which we make the world holy. Fear desecrates, profanes, curses the world, and ultimately seeks to destroy it. Approached consciously, however, fear prompts us, through our inner capacities of imagination, to create something beautiful. (Sardello, *Facing the World With Soul*, 1992)

Oddly enough, our fears are the doorway into our own redemption.

Give It a Name and It Exists

How then to cross that bridge? The beginning place, as the above passage suggests, is to make our psychopathologies holy. This hasn't, however, been predominantly the case for modern psychology. If symptoms could be isolated and grouped, a syndrome could be declared and named. Such is the coagulation upon which modern psychology and psychiatry builds its edifices. The syndrome *syndrome* (not a typo) began to intensify its mission with the advent of the 19th century, a repository of the arrival of the Age of Reason in which the compulsion to classify, organize, categorize, systemize, and regulate became a sanctioned academic and scientific pursuit. It was an era spellbound by the order and splendor of living in a clockwork cosmos.

The actual word *psychology* surfaces in the mid-1500s in perfect tandem with the Reformation. Within three centuries, mania, hypochondria and melancholia, once used to describe soul states as they pertained to a larger religious backdrop, became almost entirely psychological in use. Other words, schizophrenia, paranoia, and dementia were modern inventions of the scientific tongue, designed to give credit to the physicians who authored them. Compiled predominantly by young German men, by the turn of the 20th century the loss of the spiritual foundation in mind was a done deal. The German doctor E. Kraepelin had authored a complete guidebook that afforded classifications in which virtually every aberration could fit.

The question is what do we do with this dilemma? There are no doubt deeply entrenched truths and pain to these psychopathologies. But how do we stop making them the enemy? How do we reconfigure and re-imagine them? How do we turn the dross into gold? Can we turn these categories—mood disorders, anxiety disorders, dissociative and somatoform disorders, personality disorders, alcoholism and substance abuse disorders, sexual and gender identity disorders, dementia, delirium and amnesic disorders, childhood and eating disorders—into something beckoning towards more than just disorder?

At this time, the advent of a Fifth World, I will be the first to presume no steady set of answers to this inquiry, but the journey begins with the right set of questions. Rather than continue to denounce the advent of modernity as the loss of soul, the question remains, why did evolution take us to this place? What are the ways to work through that evolution toward more pronounced states of awareness? What is the modern's healing? Again, what seems to be asked of us is an understanding, bothcutural and psychological, of all that we as a species have been.

The Tibetan Experiment

This integration, a traversing of all of the worlds, can be tracked in a number of expressions, both East and West. Vajrayana Buddhism, the Way of the Thunderbolt, has been the bold and seasoned thousand-year attempt of Tibet to synthesize all of the Worlds: Bon shamanism, Theravadin, and Mahayana Buddhism, the Tantric ways of India, the clear Zen-like insights of Dzogchen, and the modern scientific worldview. The Dalai Lama, Vajrayana's eloquent spokesperson and global leader, has readily conceded that if modern science in any way disproves Buddhist truths, he will honor the scientific truths.

These varied strata of culture and time don't try to outrank or disqualify the others, but rather are apprehended as complementary forces. The older shamanism, the Hindu-drenched Tantra, and Buddhism's contemplative journey intelligently meld. It's as if you put on earth a worshipping disco dancer, an imagery driven Jungian psychologist, a determined Buddhist meditator, and a laboratory scientist in the same room and tell them to make a religion.

Ironically, the attempt of Communist China to snuff out this Shangri-la culture only spreads it around the world. The Vajrayana, this marvelous and uncanny forerunner to the Fifth World, has become the world's fastest growing Buddhist religion. The Dalai Lama is perhaps the world's most known and revered religious (unlike the institution of the Pope, which is not always so revered) the planet now knows.

He has made several trips to the American Southwest and found close affinity with the Pueblo peoples. He has participated in their rituals. Many of the ancient peoples ending up on the Colorado Plateau may have originated from the Tibetan one. There is a vital connection here across time and space, a connection linked by both spiritual themes and possible ancient migration.

🔀 Culture of the Southwest
The Modern Healer/Curandera

A parallel journey to Tibetan Buddhism can be tracked in the life of the *curandera* in Northern New Mexico. The wise, old healer that got wiped out with the Inquisition in Old Europe survives, amazingly, in the escape to the New World. But curanderas are not what they used to be. It is not so much that they have become New Age as that the general populace, in its exasperation with a stubborn modern medical system, has been willing to consider Old World. Combining the beliefs and practices of a pagan-saturated, medieval Christianity with an exposure to Native American and New World African healing systems, *curanderismo* is a five-hundred-year-old medical methodology and technology that spans all Four Worlds as it opens to the possibilities of a Fifth.

The life and work of Elena Avila, publishing one of the few complete books on this ancient art, and with whom I've done personal work, embodies this emergence. Trained as a registered nurse with a Master's degree in Psychiatric Nursing, Avila's turn to curanderismo came amidst her training in the biomedical paradigm. Asked to provide a report on the subject, her inquiry opened the doors for a lifelong exploration and training within her own Mayan-Zapotec-Aztec-Spanish heritage.

What Avila found was that the cultural genre of *mestizo*, which had so often been a source of denial and shame, could now become an expansive source for healing. Studying first with people in the El Paso-Juarez area where she had grown up, Avila then pursued apprenticeships with healers in Mexico and Peru. While the heart of her work contains traditional Aztec concepts of physical and spiritual health, her approach and breadth of knowledge reflects both the eclectic spread that curanderismo has become and the world medicine (the mix of the most ancient and new, of East and West) that the Fifth World is quintessentially about.

Avila does not reject modern medicine and, indeed, advises many of her acute patients to stay in or go back into the system. What Avila rejects, and why she herself had to get out of that system, is how the left-brain ways (linear, oriented on symptom and physical manifestation) dominates, represses, and/or ignores the right brain possibilities (energy flow and blockage, soul loss and trauma).

Elena Avila

It is not enough to heal the body. One must heal the wounded soul as well.

241

Avila states:

> It is not enough to heal the body. One must heal the wound-
> ed soul as well. When a person is raped, or injured in an au-
> tomobile accident, or a woman has an abortion, the physical
> scars may go away, but the scars on the soul do not. Trauma
> causes a part of the soul to get frightened away into hiding.
> When this happens, a part of our energy is no loner accessible
> to us. We need 100 percent of our soul's energy to be in good
> physical health, mental, and spiritual health...The curandera
> understands this concept of illness and has a knowledge of
> how to guide the patient back to balance. (Avila, *Woman Who
> Glows In The Dark*, 1998)

Practicing medicine is, by its intrinsic nature, soul work.

So does that mean that one has to believe and immerse oneself in the ancient symbolic worlds of the curandera to effect a cure?
Avila insists otherwise. She goes to where her patient is and only
invokes her own symbols and objects of prayer for drawing together her own strengths, or to the extent that a client might resonate
with them.

> If my patient is a seventy-year old Catholic grandmother, I
> draw her attention to the images of Jesus and the Virgin Mary
> on my altar. I don't intimidate her by lecturing to her about
> Aztec philosophies of spirit and soul. If my client is an An-
> glo lawyer who does not feel comfortable about personifying
> God, I talk about universal energy. If the patient is a woman
> who is uncomfortable with masculine concepts of divinity,
> we might talk about the three images that are painted on the
> screen behind my altar, the Virgin of Guadalupe, the Moon,
> and Coyolxauqui, the Aztec Cosmic Mother. (Avila 1998)

The curandera goes to the archetypes already activated in the patient. From that juncture, the curandera invokes contemplative
prayer. Like the Tibetan journey, all the worlds are being traversed.
The healing comes from their skilled integration.

Arrival of the Fifth World

The Fifth World is the opportunity for humanity to look back at all that we've have been, remove our blinders, and begin to integrate the best of all worlds. It all sounds rather idealistic and drastically hopeful, but this is the apocalyptic edge our technologies of war, environmental risk, and economic precariousness have pushed us towards. This kind of tension is how evolution moves forward.

The proposition is this: All the forces of history's ritual and meditation and psychological techniques are at our disposal. They are the psyche's deep domain. This may, of course, seem all too overwhelming and nebulous, but the psyche itself, the combination of imagery and emotion it continually throws at us, is the rudder in this storm. The only major obstacle is our own fundamentalism, the human flaw that we *dictate* rather than *listen to* what our next path of thought and action might be. To move past this flaw *is* the Fifth World.

There was a time when what industrialized countries have called the Third World, the lands and cultures of underdeveloped societies, was an exotic plane trip away. It has since moved next door. These are the migrations the Hopi prophecies have talked about, the unprecedented intermingling of tribal, agrarian, and industrialized peoples and ways of living on the planet.

Again, it can all seem rather confusing and overwhelming when approached via the chaos of the outer world. The industrialized world has thrown a cloak on all of us, the ancient social and infrastructures pulled out from under. But the way a people think and feel worship won't change so easily. It is too embedded into our physiological hardwiring.

Indeed, it is the same commercial outer crassness and chaos of the modern world that invites us to dive perilously inwards, to intrinsically trust the psyche that seems all too indefensibly permeable. It lets everything in and asks us to ponder it. This seeming vulnerability is also its strength. Why? Because whatever comes by

243

way of the psyche, the psyche will always try to restore balance.

The problem and challenge is that many of us moderns have not been trained, or raised in a culture that cultivates, an understanding of the psyche's clues. Screaming for attention, for the modern, is the return of the feminine after a 5,000-year societal submersion.

Personal Journey

My stuff, my family's stuff, my culture's stuff, belongs to the stuff of the world. There's not a whole lot I can directly do to remedy that history, but the continual personal quest was that I come to know it. This, then, is what I had to do. I had to go back to the ancient archetypal Wotan figure in the Seneca Hills and introduce him to Christ in a new way, to sooth the discord the Christian culture and Inquisition imposed on these ancient pagan Gods. Wotan no longer has to be this angry driven force that fueled the likes of the Nazi regime. He returns to be the stern, wise old man figure that can comfortably fold into, rather than be persecuted by, the Christ force to come.

In order to achieve this, I had to go back and forgive and reintegrate history. In so doing, miraculously, I could now, once again, experience the struggles of my psyche as really having little to do with me (which, of course, the ego assumes). This was simply the tide of history being passed down, from generation to generation, from parent to child, from sibling to sibling. The one important piece missing is this surging return of the feminine.

Crones, wise women, have been showing up in my psyche all of my life largely through my dreams. A few stand out. My maternal grandmother chomping on a cigar, a sign of power in the Afro-Caribbean expressions I have been immersed in, a clear retrieval of the power modern culture had stripped from her.

In another dream, a grandmother figure: a Native American elder cleaning out the carcass of a deer, a New World Kali figure.

Destruction is life. Death is rebirth. But it was a dream of a living divine mother that brought my healing full circle.

I'm back in junior high school; my mother, sister, and I are in attendance at some kind of school function. Ammachi (Mata Amritanandamayi) shows up, the Divine Mother figure of India, who makes yearly pilgrimages to New Mexico in her tours around the world. She is there to deliver *Darshan*, the hugs and blessings, the eternal, omnipresent mother we've all wanted.

Ammachi

She is there to deliver Darshan, the hugs and blessings, the eternal, omnipresent mother we've all wanted.

In the dream, her energy is, at once, "no bullshit now" and pure love. After all, beneath her total sweetness was the complete devotion to and guidance from Kali, the Goddess of destruction. Once again, without death, there is no life. In the dream we speak. She shares her passion for poetry, an indication of the many different creative expressions we humans have for the divine.

Spirituality, the spark that sets all religion into motion and creed, may be none other than this: spirituality as the simple appreciation of beauty in its myriad forms. This may be either in actual creative endeavor, or in simply seeing and experiencing the world in aesthetic wonder. It is those endeavors—a word, an utterance, a poem, a song, a chant, a painting on caves or canvas, a dance—that inform and remind us of the transcendent splendor that the world truly is. And then there is something uncanny about how, wherever two or more are gathered, that enhances and deepens the power of that experience.

After the gathering, Ammachi and I mull into a crowd and the Divine Mother whispers, letting me know that we don't have to meet for a family meeting. I know upon awakening the instant meaning: the mother and father issues that many of us in industrial culture carry with our rampant loss of community and family were coming to an end. Ammachi's presence allows me to forgive the familial wounding that came streaming down through industrial culture. As in the mother earth and father sky dynamics of indigenous culture, a new set of parents shine forth

And so there I was, in real life, sitting by my father's deathbed, my mother and sister also in attendance. The healing potential of this dream was now fully evident. I have nothing but love in my heart. I had just flown in from across the country, my father not conscious but clearly struggling in his unconscious state with the imminent loss of his life.

I seized his hand and prayed, as is my way these days, into him through my dear Lord and Savior Christ Jesus. As is his nature, when Jesus comes into the room, we all burst into tears. This vigil continued for two more days, with evening breaks. My father, in what psychology erroneously calls a state of dementia, was recapitulating his life, drawn back into the journey of his psyche that produced all of his joys and worries.

My mother would later ask me what I was doing and I said I was praying. We, as did many a modern family and individual, went screaming away from organized religion, because of its social-ly coercive elements. My family was cynically content being secular humanists.

But it was precisely this critical thinking that allowed me to reenter the cultural journey of religion and find the silver linings ev-ery step of the way. After my adventures into indigenous, Eastern, and Sufi ritual, it was only natural that I would arrive and settle at the Christ. This was the religious figure whose churches based on his teachings turned both my parents away from religion.

But I, in my exploration, was able to find the redemptive piece. The Jesus that I met was not one that came into opposition to all that came before, but honored the way of the Christ that was alive in all ways. My ecumenical journey was not unique. Martin Luther King nominated a little known Buddhist monk, Thich Nhat Hanh, for the Nobel Peace Prize back in 1968, and who has since become one of the planet's greatest Buddhist teachers. Bishop Carl-ton Pearson, who was at the top of the top of the Pentecostal world, was revealed *The Gospel of Inclusion* (2006). He was promptly de-clared a heretic, lost everything he had, but has since become even more known to the world for his revelation. Today's heretic is to-morrow's prophet.

And so on the third day, my father awoke, greeting me with a smile and a hug that will light up my memories the rest of my days. He had come back to say goodbye with a kind of regal elegance. The torment was gone. Even though he was a nonbeliever, I can't help but feel and wonder that in the channel of love that connected us as father and son, the Christ rode in on my prayers. My father passed a few days later, much more at peace.

My father's family lost everything in the Great Depression of the 1930s. After my father passed, the market began to crash again, threatening all that he had made so his family could be secure when he was gone. My father later showed up in a dream, anxious and distraught that this was happening. I assured him in the dream, as a message to equally assure myself, that everything was going to be all right.

Conclusion: Iyeska

We are all mestizo. We are all mixed blood. Actually, always have been. The researcher for ethnic purity finds little. Like peeling layers of an onion, there's nothing at the end of that search but a continual mixing and matching of peoples. Exogamy is the first rule of culture. Marry out of your clan, strengthen the gene pool, and make an alliance with the peoples across the way.

Ten years ago, I had the opportunity to be a part of an "indigenous" gathering with Maori elders on New Zealand's north island. In contemplating going, I questioned the organizer Kaylynn TwoTrees, a life-long teacher for me, whether as a third generation American and half German Jew, half German Baptist, I belonged in an indigenous gathering. Her response was, "I belonged if I felt like I did." We are all, after all, indigenous to the earth.

The initial name Kaylynn has given to her endeavors is *Iyeska*, a (Lakota) Sioux word for "mixed blood." More so than ever, this is who we now are on the planet. The more we appreciate and explore this, the more evident the purpose of our journey becomes.

Amidst our first gathering in Auckland, a warrior-clad Maori man ran at us at full speed with spear in hand and tongue extended. The idea was here is my tribe's spirit and strength for you to fully see and experience. What is yours? The ritual instruction was this: Each of us was to share our clan history, our father's clan, our mother's clan, and the land and water forms indigenous to these clans and our upbringing. We then culminated with breaking bread.

A subsequent weeklong ritual occurred up north by the ocean's side. We were a motley collection of Europeans, Americans, and the Maori. The Maori, themselves, are now a mixture of varied amounts of European blood. There we were in the Maori meeting house, all sleeping, breathing, dreaming, and sharing under one roof. Every night we would assemble after dinner and begin a talking circle. All prayers, chants, thoughts, psychological drama, silence were welcome.

You'd think after a few hours we'd run out of things to say, but this went on for five nights, never ending before one or two in the morning. While many of us would drift into sleep, the elders held the space at the front, always mindful, always attentive, to whoever was sharing. I experienced the exact same kind of attentiveness with a Huichol grandmother, perched behind her eagle feathers, as she took in the stories and vibrations of a multicultural overnight peyote gathering. At the end of each evening, they would sum up the stories, the Maori elders, just like the Huichol grandmother, in their wisdom, making one story out of all of them. After all, that's all there really is to this journey. The human story.

Kaylynn TwoTrees

I questioned Kaylynn Twotrees, a life-long teacher for me, whether as a third generation American and half German Jew, half German Baptist, I belonged in an indigenous gathering. Her response was "I belonged if I felt like I did." We are all, after all, indigenous to the earth.

⊡ Practical Applications

Most of us in the course of our life try to strike a balance between meeting our needs and serving something greater than ourselves. No matter what the snares that may befall or challenge are, most of us have an intuitive vision of how we want to live. Due to the particular nature of where humanity culturally is now, that vision necessarily beckons towards a Fifth World. There is no culture untainted by another type of culture, and most of us have traversed several. Our strategies for survival and wellbeing are necessarily multicultural.

What appear to be our greatest historical struggles and deepest psychological complexes carry within themselves the seeds of their own reconciliation. Some of these struggles and complexes we may make peace with, some we may take to our graves. But either way, reconciliation is the inherent hope and light that the psyche and the global wisdom traditions hold out for us. This reconciliation, in a way that the planet is only beginning to realize, promises a healing between and for all of the Worlds.

When I ask my students and clients about what the future has in store for us, most share a combination of hope and dread, of the best laid plans for a meaningful life and the fear that those aspirations won't come to fruition. The greatest challenge often seems to be just being able to hang out with the not knowing.

Therapeutic applications are about becoming familiar and skilled with the ways and therapeutic applications of all of the previous Worlds, and knowing when and how to apply them. For those born into World Five, which essentially means any of us willing to go there, this is a time of tremendous apocalyptic pressures, but the gifts of grace are equally at hand.

In the final analysis, this is the story of the author's first client, himself. At first, a young man, and now a middle aged man, who always seemed to find himself in terrible binds. The mind seemed to work like this constant binary trap. Whatever thought or feeling would pop up, an opposing one would surface to meet it. Finally, in his midlife years, this all began to exhaust him. Something had to shift.

The dreams, as dreams tend to do, came to the rescue. While generally abhorred by the latest of America's wars, in the dream he is hired as an anthropological consultant for the Iraq conflict and treated by the military with nothing but courtesy and respect. The next dream: Meeting up with a man, who in real life always treated him like some indulgent Jungian weakling. In the dream the man expresses awe and respect for this very piece of writing. And finally his father, though entrenched in his life in worldly endeavor, in the dream has a deep sharing with his son amidst ancient Native ruins.

The lesson is clear. The tension of the opposites, the polarities—fundamentalist/ecumenical, Democrat/Republican, love/distrust—will continue to confuse and irritate until a detached, wiser consciousness emerges that soars beyond these dichotomies. The dreams—the soul, this collective unconscious—will work out on an energetic level what reality cannot. There's no way around the fire but through it. In this meeting of fire with fire, our conviction becomes matched with a resolve that is not unsettled by the tension that comes our way. Therein lies the grace.

World Five Summary

As the overwhelming majority of our time on the planet was spent within shamanic cultures (Worlds One and Two), there's a biological and cultural hardwiring here that will always point us in a shamanic direction. As has been a central thesis in *Apocalyptic Grace,* the later spiritual expressions, most notably the World Religions, really amount to forms of evolved shamanism. All of the World's cultural citizens are so much more alike than we are different.

World Five is about consciously returning to and integrating these roots, not through anthropological adventures to more ancient cultures (although that can help), but by understanding that the journey inside is like a march through time. Assisting us on this journey are many of the techniques of modern psychology (visualization, active imagination, journaling, dream analysis), many of which have their genesis in these ancient worlds.

Navigating this journey in World Four felt a bit like voyeurism; many of us felt out of place and inept at diving into these deeper, ancestral Worlds. World Five rewards us at having becoming more adept at that journey, and having teachings and teachers more available that can help guide the way.

Global Archetypal Unfolding
The Future Was Yesterday

The possibilities of planetary unity beyond race, religion, and creed are forecasted in all of the previous Worlds. The early part of the 21st century poses the *apocalyptic* opportunity to bring that Vision ever more alive.

The Great Awakenings

The United States, in its stumbling imperialism and ethnocentrism inherent to World Four, always held forth, and was renown for, this Vision of Unity. Three historical "Awakenings" demonstrate this country trying to become more conscious of its true mission.

Give It a Name and It Exists

The modern world tends to get overwhelmed by the magnitude of its dysfunction and pathology. This section suggests that these abnormalities are the invitation into a greater awareness and, ultimately, peace.

The Tibetan Experiment

Tibet's Vajrayana Buddhism is presented as an example that peacefully integrated all of these Worlds.

顓 Culture of the Southwest
The Modern Healer / Curandera

The modern day curandera, in the life and work of Elena Avila, is presented as an example of a kind of healer and healing that traverses all of these Worlds.

Arrival of the Fifth World

This is a summation of the entire book. Now is the opportunity to step back into an awareness of the kinds of consciousness that shamanic, agrarian and industrial culture afforded us, and thus to be able to step into a truly unifying multicultural consciousness.

꽃 Personal Journey

An account of a family healing dream I had with the Divine Mother Ammachi. I, then, share the prayerful experience I had with these same members of my family while beside my father's deathbed.

Conclusion: Iyeska

A sharing of a ritual gathering I experienced with my friend and teacher Kaylynn TwoTrees that fully captures what the Fifth World is about.

 Practical Applications

The final counseling lesson, particularly for myself, is learning how to move beyond polarity and opposition. This applies not only to interactions in the world, but foremost, to move beyond the "binary trap" the mind continually poses. Therein lies the eternal grace.

TEN EXPLORATIONS FOR ENGAGING THE FIVE WORLDS WITHIN

World One - Foraging Culture

1. What visions have you had that connected you to your life purpose? What archetypes (*i.e.,* warrior, sage, seeker, lover) were involved?

2. How are myth (belief systems) and ritual operating in your life?

World Two - Tribal Farming Culture

3. How have group experiences, wherever two or more are gathered, created a kind of tribal support for you?

4. How have group experiences been challenging?

World Three - Agrarian Hierarchal Culture

5. Where in your cultural background are there examples of those who have been oppressed and those who have been oppressors? How is this related to how you have been discriminated against and discriminated against others?

6. What is your relationship, positive and negative, to one or more of the World Religions?

World Four—Industrial Culture

7. This is about examining the breakdown of extended family and community the industrial world created. What has been the impact, both positive and negative, of your family and community of origin? How have you been able to recreate family and community?

8. What have been the positive and challenging aspects of having free choice, the core value of industrial culture, in your life?

World Five — A World without Borders

9. In what ways are you in touch with the cultures and ways of the previous four Worlds?

10. Your awareness of the expanding multicultural dynamics around and within you is the way of the Fifth World. What is your vision of the Fifth World?

Bibliography

Armstrong, Karen 2007. *The Great Transformation: The Beginning of Our Religious Traditions*. New York: Knopf Publishing Group.

Avila, E. 1998. *Woman Who Glows in the Dark: A Curandera Reveals Traditional Aztec Secrets of Physical and Spiritual Health*. New York: J.P. Tarcher.

Balfour, M. 1990. *The Sign of the Serpent - The Key to Creative Physics*. Great Britain: Prism Press.

Beck, W. 1969. *Modern Science and the Nature of Life*. New York: Wadsworth.

Bly, Robert 1992. *A Little Book on the Human Shadow*. San Francisco: Harper.

Berger, Peter, and T. Luckmann 1967. *The Social Construction of Reality*. Garden City, NY: Anchor Books.

Bourgeault, Cynthia 2008. *The Wisdom Jesus: Transforming Heart and Mind - a New perspective on Christ and His Message*. Boston & London: Shambala.

Braud, W. and R. Anderson 1998. *Transpersonal Research Methods for the Social Sciences: Honoring Human Experience*. Thousand Oaks: Sage Publications.

Brown, Norman 1966. *Love Body*. New York: Vintage.

Cajete, G. 2000. *Native Science: Natural Laws of Interdependence*. Santa Fe, NM: Clear Light Publishers.

Campbell, J. 1959. *The Masks of God: Primitive Mythology*. New York: Viking.

———. 1972. *The Hero with a Thousand Faces*. Princeton, NJ: Princeton University Press.

Carotenuto, A. 1981. *The Vertical Labyrinth: Individuation in Jungian Psychology*. Toronto, Canada: Inner City Books.

Cook, M. 2005. *A Brief History of the Human Race*. New York: W. W. Norton & Company.

Corbett, L. 1996. *The Religious Function of the Psyche*. London: Routledge.

Corey, G. 1995. *Theory and Practice of Group Counseling, 5th Edition*. Pacific Grove, CA: Brooks/Cole.

Coward, H. G. 1985. Jung and Eastern Thought. Albany, NY: SUNY Press.

Danielou, A. 1984. *Shiva and Dionysus: The Omnipresent Gods of Transcendence and Ecstasy*. New York: East-West Publications.

Debus, A. 1977. *The Chemical Philosophy: Paracelsian Medicine in the 16th and 17th Centuries, Vols. 1 & 2*. New York: Science History Publications.

Deloria Jr., Vine 1973. *God is Red*. New York: Dell Publishing.

Diagnostic and Statistical Manual of Mental Disorders DSM-IV-TR. Fourth Edition 2000. Washington, DC: American Psychiatric Association.

Easlea, B. 1980. *Witchhunting, Magic and the New Philosophy: An Introduction to the Debates of the Scientific Revolution*. Sussex, London: The Harvester Press.

———. 1963. *Myth and Reality*. New York: Harper and Row.

———. 1964. *Shamanism: Archaic Techniques of Ecstasy*. Princeton, NJ: Princeton University Press.

———. 1978. *A History of Religious Ideas*. Chicago: The University of Chicago Press.

Edinger, Edward F. 1999. *Archetype of the Apocalypse: Divine Vengeance, Terrorism, and the End of the World*. Peru, IL: Open Court Publishing.

———. 1987. *The Christian Archetype: A Jungian Commentary of the Life of Christ and ego and Self*. Studies in Jungian Psychology by Jungian Analysts, Vol. 28.

Elizondo, V. 1997. *Guadalupe: Mother of the New Creation*. New York: Orbis Books.

Epstein, M. 1998. *Going to Pieces Without Falling Apart: Lessons From Meditation and Psychotherapy.* New York: Broadway Books.

Feuerstein, G. 1987. *Structures of Consciousness: The Genius of Jean Gebser.* California: Integral Publishing.

Fideler, David 1993. *Jesus Christ, Sun of God: Ancient Cosmology and Early Christian Symbolism.* Wheaton, IL: Quest Books.

Fieser, James and J. Powers 2004. *Scriptures of the East.* New York: McGraw-Hill.

Fisher, Mary 2002. *Living Religions.* New Jersey: Prentice Hall.

Foster, S. and M. Little 1999. *The Four Shields: The Initiatory Seasons of Human Nature.* Big Pine, CA: Lost Borders Press.

Foucault, Michael 1980. *Power/Knowledge: Selected Interviews and Other Writings.* New York: Pantheon Books.

———. 1965. *Madness and Civilization: A History of Insanity in the Age of Reason.* New York: Vintage Books.

Gebser, J. 1986. *The Ever-Present Origin.* Athens, OH: Ohio University Press.

Gerber, R. 1988. *Vibrational Medicine.* Santa Fe, NM: Bear & Company.

Gimbutas, Marija 1982. *Goddesses and Gods of Old Europe, 6,500-3,500 BC: Myth and Cult Image.* Los Angeles: University of California Press.

Grof, C. and S. Grof 1990. *The Stormy Search for the Self: A Guide to Personal Growth through Transformational Crisis.* Los Angeles: Jeremy P. Tarcher, Inc.

Gutierrez, R. 1991. *When Jesus Came, The Corn Mothers Went Away: Marriage, Sexuality, and Power in New Mexico, 1500-1846.* Stanford, CA: Stanford University Press.

Hannah, Barbara 1991. *Jung: His Life and Work.* Boston: Shambala.

Hillman, James 1972. *The Myth of Analysis: Three Essays in Archetypal Psychology*. New York: Harper Torchbooks.

———. 1975. *Re-Visioning Psychology*. New York: Harper & Row.

Hirst, P. and P. Wooley 1982. *Social Relations and Human Attributes*. London: Tavistock Publications.

Hollis, J. 1994. *Under Saturn's Shadow: The Wounding and Healing of Men*. Toronto, Canada: Inner City Books.

Houston, Jean 1993. *Life Force: The Psycho-Historical Recovery of the Self*. Wheaton, IL: Quest Books.

Huxley, Aldous 2004. *The Perennial Philosophy*. New York: Harper Collins.

Jacobi, Jolande 1942. *The Psychology of C. G. Jung*. New Haven, CT: Yale University Press.

Jung, Carl Gustav 1938. *Psychology and Religion*. New Haven, CT: Yale University Press.

———. 1960. *On the Nature of the Psyche*. New York: Bollingen.

———. 1973. *Answer to Job*. New York: Bollingen.

———. 1978. *Psychology and the East*. New York: Bollingen.

———. 1986. *Essays on Contemporary Events*. New York: Bollingen.

Kavanaugh, K. and R. Kavanaugh, trans. 1991. *The Collected Works of Saint John of the Cross*. Washington: ICS Publications.

Keeney, Bradford 2007. *Shaking Medicine: The Healing Power of Ecstatic Movement*. Rochester, NY: Destiny Books.

Keith-Spiegel, P. and G. P. Koocher 1995. *Ethics in Psychology: Professional Standards and Cases*. Hillsdale, NJ: Lawrence Erlbaum Associates.

King, S. 1985. *Mastering Your Hidden Self: A Guide to the Huna Way*. Wheaton, IL: Quest Books.

Keating, T. 1986. *Open Mind, Open Heart: The Contemplative Dimension of the Gospel*. New York: Continuum.

Kottak, C. P. 2002. *Cultural Anthropology*. New York: McGraw-Hill.

LaBarre, W. 1978. *The Ghost Dance: The Origins of Religion.* New York: Dell Publishing.

———. 1971. *The Peyote Cult.* New York: Schocken Books.

Lévy-Bruhl, Lucien 1926. *How Natives Think.* Lilian A. Clare, trans. London: George Allen and Unwin, Ltd.

Levi-Strauss, C. 1979. *Myth and Meaning.* New York: Schocken.

Lovelock, James 1995. *The Ages of Gaia: A Biography of Our Living Earth.* New York: Norton.

———. 2000. *Gaia: A New Look at Life on Earth.* Oxford, England: Oxford University Press.

Matthews, J. and C. Matthews 1985. *The Western Way: A Practical Guide to the Western Mystery Tradition.* London: Arkana.

Mazour, A., J. Peoples, and T. Rabb 1983. *People and Nations – A World History.* Orlando, FL: Harcourt Press.

Merriam-Webster's Collegiate Dictionary 7th edition 1967. Springfield, IL: Merriam-Webster.

Miller, I. and R. Miller 1994. *The Modern Alchemist: A Guide to Personal Transformation.* Grand Rapids, MI: Phanes Press.

Mindell, Arnold 1985. *River's Way: The Process Science of the Dreambody.* London: Arkana.

———. 1992. *The Leader as Martial Artist: An Introduction to Deep Democracy.* San Francisco: Harper.

———. 1993. *The Shaman's Body: A New Shamanism for Transforming Health, Relationships, and the Community.* San Francisco: Harper.

———. 1995. *Sitting in the Fire: Large Group Transformation Using Conflict and Diversity.* Portland, OR: LaoTse Press.

Minuchin, Salvador, W. Lee, and G. M. Simon 1996. *Mastering Family Therapy: Journeys of Growth and Transformation.* New York: John Riley & Sons.

Mooney, James 1991. *The Ghost-Dance Religion and Wounded Knee.* New York: Courier Dover Publications.

Moore, R. 2001. *The Archetype of Initiation: Sacred Space, Ritual Process, and Personal Transformation.* Villa Park, IL: New World Community Books.

Moore, R. and D. Gillette 1990. *King, Warrior, Lover, Magician: Rediscovering the Archetypes of the Mature Masculine Personality.* New York: Harper Collins.

Moore, Thomas 1992. *Care of the Soul: A Guide for Cultivating Depth and Sacredness in Everyday Life.* New York: HarperCollins.

———. 2004. *Dark Nights of the Soul: A Guide to Finding Your Way Through Life's Ordeals.* New York: Gotham.

Moustakis, C. 1990. *Heuristic research: Design, Methodology, and Applications.* Newbury Park, NJ: Sage Publications.

Neumann, Erich 1954. *The Origins and History of Consciousness.* Princeton, NJ: Princeton University Press.

Noble, David G. 1989. *Santa Fe: History of an Ancient City.* Santa Fe, NM: School of Advanced Research Press.

Noss, David 2007. *A History of the World's Religions.* New York: Prentice Hall.

Novick, R. 1999. *Fundamentals of Tibetan Buddhism.* Freedom, CA: The Crossing Press.

Pagel, W. 1958. *Paracelsus: An Introduction to Philosophical medicine in the Era of the Renaissance.* Switzerland: Basel-Karger.

Pagels, Elaine. 1979. *The Gnostic Gospels.* New York: Vintage Books.

Pearson, Carlton 2006, *The Gospel of Inclusion: Reaching Beyond Religious Fundamentalism to the True Love of God.* New York: Atria.

Petersen, S. 1999. *Native American Prophecies.* New York: Continuum International Publishing Group.

Poling-Kempes, Leslie 1997. *Valley of Shining Stone: The Story of Abiquiu.* Tuscon, AZ: University of Arizona Press.

Powell, Stephen 1988. *Dread Rites: An Account of Rastafarian Music and Ritual Process in Popular Culture.* Montreal, Canada: McGill University.

———. 1995. "All Groan Up." *The Santa Fe Sun*, Vol. 7, no. 3.

———. 1996. "A Conversation with Bly." *The Santa Fe Sun*, Vol. 8, no. 11, 13.

———. 1997. "Can We Get Along?" *The Santa Fe Sun*, Vol. 9, no. 3, 7.

———. 1998. "The Red Road Goes Pop." *Four Corners Magazine*, August/September, 6-9.

———. 1999. "Performance Melds Ancients, Modern Sacred Ideas." *The Santa Fe New Mexican.* Vol. 33, no. 7.

———. 2000. "Saving our Sacred Marriage." *Salt Journal: Reconstructing Meaning*, Vol. 2, no. 4, 39-44.

Publication Manual of the American Psychological Association. 2001. Washington, DC: American Psychological Association.

Roberts, S. and C. Roberts 1988. *New Mexico.* Albuquerque, NM: University of New Mexico Press.

Riley, Gregory 1997. *One Jesus, Many Christs.* San Francisco: Harper.

Sardello, Robert 1992. *Facing the World with Soul: The Reimagination of Modern Life.* Hudson, New York: Lindisfarne Press.

———. 1999. *Freeing the Soul from Fear.* New York: Riverhead Books.

Sebastian, Lynne 1992. *The Chaco Anasazi.* Cambridge, England: Cambridge University Press.

Sheldrake, Rupert 2000. *Dogs That Know When Their Owners Are Coming Home: And Other Unexplained Powers of Animals.* London: Three Rivers Press.

Shalit, E. 2002. *The Complex Path of Transformation from Archetype to Ego.* Toronto, Canada: Inner City Books.

Sharp, D. 1998. *Jungian Psychology Unplugged.* Toronto, Canada: Inner City Books.

Shlain, Leonard 1998. *The Alphabet Versus the Goddess: The Conflict between Word and Image*. New York: Penguin.

Suzuki, S. 1973. *Zen Mind, Beginner's Mind*. New York: Weatherhill.

Szasz, T. S. 1971. *The Myth of Mental Illness*. New York: Hoeber.

Shoumatoff, A. 1997. *Legends of the American Desert: Sojourns in the Greater Southwest*. New York: Alfred A. Knopf.

Small, J. 1982. *Transformers: Personal Transformation: The Way Through*. Marina del Rey, CA: DeVorss & Co.

Smoley, R. and J. Kinney 1999. *Hidden Wisdom: A Guide to the Western Inner Traditions*. New York: Penguin/Arkana.

Sue, Derald Wing and David Sue 2003. *Counseling the Culturally Diverse: Theory and Practice, 4th Edition*. New York: Wiley & Sons.

Tarnas, R. 1993. *The Passion of the Western Mind: Understanding the Ideas that Have Shaped Our World View*. New York: Ballantine.

Taylor, Eugene 1999. *Shadow Culture: Psychology and Spirituality in America*. Washington: Counterpoint.

Taylor, K. 1995. *The Ethics of Caring: Honoring the Web of Life in Our Professional Healing Relationships*. Santa Cruz, CA: Hanford Mead Publications.

Trevor-Roper, Hugh R. 1969. *The European Witch-Craze of the 16th and 17th Centuries and Other Essays*. New York: Harper & Row.

Turner, Victor 1969. *The Ritual Process: Structure and Anti-Structure*. Ithaca, NY: Cornell University Press.

———. 1982. *From Ritual to Theatre: The Human Seriousness of Play*. New York: Performing Arts Journal Publication.

Utter, J. 1993. *American Indians: Answers to Today's Questions*. Michigan: National Woodlands Publishing Company.

Wallace, Anthony 1956. *Revitalization Movements*. American Anthropologist 58: 264-281.

Waterman, R. D. 2001. *Through the Eyes of Soul: Theory and Practice of Noetic Field Therapy*. Santa Fe, NM: International Mystery School.

Waters, Frank 1963. *Book of the Hopi*. New York: Penguin.

Watkins, Alfred 1925. *The Old Straight Track: Its Mounds, Beacons, Moats, Sites, and Mark Stones*. England: Methuen.

Weber, Max 1958. *The Protestant Ethic and the Spirit of Capitalism*. New York: Scribner.

Welwood, J. 2000. *Toward a Psychology of Awakening: Buddhism, Psychotherapy and the Path of Personal and Spiritual Transformation*. Boston: Shambala.

Werner, Craig 1999. *A Change Is Gonna Come: Music, Race and The Soul of America*. New York: Plume.

Whitmont, E. C. 1969. *The Symbolic Quest: Basic Concepts of Analytical Psychology*. Englewood Cliffs, NJ: Princeton University Press.

Wilber, Ken 1996. *The Atman Project: A Transpersonal View of Human Development*. Wheaton, IL: Quest Books.

———. 1996. *A Brief History of Everything*. Boston: Shambala.

———. 1998. *The Marriage of Sense and Soul*. New York: Broadway Books.

Woodman, Marion and E. Dickson 1996. *Dancing in the Flames: The Dark Goddess in the Transformation of Consciousness*. Boston: Shambala Publications.

Yogananda, Paramahansa 2006. *Autobiography of a Yogi*. Los Angeles: Self Realization Fellowship Publishing.

———. 2004. *The Second Coming of Christ: The Resurrection of the Christ Within You: A Revelatory Commentary on the Original Teachings of Jesus*. Los Angeles: Self-Realization Fellowship Publishing.

Index

About the Author

Stephen Powell is a Licensed Mental Health Counselor (LMHC) and holds masters degrees in Cultural Anthropology from McGill University and Counseling Psychology from Prescott College. He graduated magna cum laude from Temple University with a degree in Comparative Religion. Powell teaches all three disciplines at the University of New Mexico, Santa Fe Community College and Northern New Mexico Community College.

As a percussionist, Powell likes to help get his clients in recovery "funked up" by leading therapeutic drum circles. He is one of the Ravens in the tribal funk band "DL and the Ravens," and has been known to "seriously get down in the name of the Lord" playing for a number of Gospel churches.